Love

Worth the Wait

Trusting God for Real Romance and Real Relationship

by Sandy Weyeneth

Published by Plum Tree Ministries
1118 War Eagle Court, Colorado Springs, Colorado, 80919

Love Worth the Wait:
Trusting God for Real Romance and Real Relationship

By Sandy Weyeneth
©2009 Sandy Weyeneth. All rights reserved. No part of this publication may be reproduced in any form without written permission from the author, Sandy Weyeneth at 1118 War Eagle Court, Colorado Springs, Colorado, 80919, or Sweyeneth@comcast.net.

ISBN 978-0-9825349-0-8

Printed in the United States of America

Unless otherwise noted, all Scriptures are taken from the HOLY BIBLE, NEW INTERNATIONAL VERSION® (NIV®). Copyright © 1973, 1978, 1984 by International Bible Society. Used by permission of Zondervan Bible Publishing House. All rights reserved. Also used is THE NEW AMERICAN STANDARD BIBLE® (NASB), © The Lockman Foundation 1960, 1962, 1963, 1968, 1971, 1973, 1975, 1977. Used by permission.

Praise for *Love Worth the Wait*

"This book reminded me that waiting is not an enemy, but space created by God to do magnificent things in the lives of His people. Courage and joy filled my heart as I witnessed God's goodness unfold in this compelling love story, restoring my hope that love really is worth the wait!"
— Lauren from Colorado

"I was captivated. This story will encourage your heart to trust the faithfulness of God, wherever that may lead you, knowing He always has our best interests in mind."
— Kathy Norquist
Executive assistant to best-selling author Randy Alcorn

"This is a must read! In a day of much confusion and compromise in relationships, here is clarity and renewed anticipation of what God can do. The practical and sage help in romance, love, and marriage comes with a warm human touch."
— Dwight Hill
Facts of the Matter.org

"Everyone loves a great love story. Love Worth the Wait *elevates and sanctifies both the waiting and the love and marriage that follow."*
— Jean Fleming
Feeding Your Soul: A Quiet Time Handbook

"This book breaks through the world's lies to reveal God's intentions for relationships. It's a timely reminder that God's promises are worth waiting for!"
— Dana from Nebraska

"This story clearly shows that blessed are they who wait for the Lord, much like Ruth and Boaz did. I also love the down-to-earth suggestions for trusting the Creator for love worth the wait."
— Bob Lewis
Capitol Ministries

Dedicated To

Coleen, a loving and inspiring friend of like heart

Contents

Acknowledgments

Thank you to several people for making this book possible. First, to my father-in-law, Rich, who shed a tear after reading some of the initial e-mail messages between Randy and me and said, "This is a beautiful story." That birthed the inspiration to put our story in print.

Thank you to Dana Herr, Julia Warton, Lauren Johnson, and Michael Bass, who read my initial draft and gave insightful feedback that greatly enhanced and shaped it. To my husband, Randy, who should write a book on how to pursue a woman! He wrote some of the content of this book. He also offered tremendous encouragement, ideas, editing, and vision.

A big thanks to Leura Jones, whose awesome editing formed this into a much better book. We're grateful that you also introduced us to wonderful people in the publishing process. Thanks to Steve Learned for the excellent book cover design and typesetting. Becky Simpson did wonderfully at proofreading. We are also grateful to Dave and Mary Dawson who encouraged us in the publishing process.

I am thankful for many friends and colleagues who have loved, mentored, and influenced both Randy and me throughout our lives. Your influence is woven into the fabric of our hearts, and thus into this story as well.

My prayer and desire for putting this story into print comes from Psalm 78:4–7. May you see the power, the wonders, and the praise-worthy deeds of the LORD so that you will put your trust in God, and not forget His deeds, but keep His commands. All praise to Him.

Introduction

Since coming to faith in college many years ago, one of my deep and ongoing desires was for real relationship. I grew tired of the other kind—relationships in which he hesitates to lead, communicates poorly, lacks emotional integrity, or is missing a true sense of living for a cause larger than his own self-interest. My desire was to communicate on a heart level, grow in trust, have similar core values, and share a motivation to impact others for good. I wanted the kind of relationship where we genuinely enjoyed each other and could seek the very best for one another.

Real relationship puts a zing in your step and a song in your heart. It makes you feel loved and cherished. It lights you up inside and encourages you in wholehearted faith and obedience to God. Yet with the confusion that comes with defining relationships these days, and the difficulty of waiting for love, how do you find genuine relationship? How do you lasso the grit and graciousness to wait for love? How do you discover the real deal that leads to "I do"?

When I was 22 years old, I had a mountain of issues and everything to learn about real relationship, but my heart felt the familiar tug for love and connection. One diary entry reveals:

"How I long for a close friend and to be able to relate to men. Sometimes I am disrespectful toward men, mostly because I don't know of too many men worth respecting. Where are our knights in shining armor . . . kind, zealous for God, genuine, strong, fun, tender? Do I have unrealistic expectations? I don't know. Sometimes I am a dip—scared of a relationship yet wanting one. I struggle with wanting to be married, but I'm glad God has protected me from my motives right now, wanting more to get instead of to give."

Embedded in my longing for love was the yearning to have a family, to serve God, and to live in a wonderful community. I came to believe that God was good, and I dearly hoped that He would give me these good things. The more I learned of God and drank in His Word, the Bible, the closer my heart was drawn and yielded to Him. Yet after several years of some dating, and many stale seasons of sparse dating, I reluctantly meandered into my late thirties with a bleak reality: I remained single with few prospects on the horizon. Not one marriage proposal had come. Where was my Prince Charming? Even more to the point, where was God in this? Isn't God supposed to reward those who seek Him?

How often when we cannot see or control things, the Lord asks us to wait, hold our desires with an open hand, and trust Him, whatever the outcome.

Over the years, sometimes my painful longing drew me to the Lord, and other times it pushed me away from Him. During some "up" days, my faith soared, and I knew that God Almighty was not limited. He could usher in real relationship and a wonderful man to marry. I believed!

On other "down" days, loneliness seared until I ached. Crying myself to sleep, I felt inadequate, left behind, and even wondered if something was wrong with me. Old, wrong ways of thinking would butt in: *"He always chooses the other girl, not you."* Deep down I wondered, *"Will a man ever love me for real? Is there love worth waiting for?"*

God had planted reason to hope for just such a thing too. When I was 26, one day I took my time reading through chapters 46–59 in Isaiah. It was powerful. Chapter 49, verses 13–23, stood out so clearly that I knew it was the Lord speaking to me. Though not audible, the Holy Spirit impressed on my spirit that *my* wedding day would be like verse 18: "Lift up your eyes and look around; all of them gather together, they come to you. . . . You shall surely put on all of them as jewels, and bind them on as a bride."

Yet I still wrestled. Was this a message from God, or was I making it into something I wanted to hear? I feared the latter. Yet as I yielded and prayed, the Holy Spirit clearly bore witness to my spirit, *"This is for you Sandy. Behold, I am going to do this for you."*

I would not meet my husband Randy for another 13 years.

In looking for love, the Lord Himself wanted to meet my needs. The Lord of heaven and earth wanted to wrap me in His bottomless, extravagant love and have first place in my heart and life. Learning to draw near to Him, to trust Him, and to walk with Him satisfied deep parts of my soul. For underneath all my layers and struggles and dreams, what I intensely desired was to be *wanted*. I wanted to be wanted, and Jesus Christ wanted a relationship with *me*. He truly loved me! As I grew in this relationship with Him, He satisfied me like no other.

As my late thirties chugged along, Jesus Christ remained my first love, but the likelihood for a real relationship and marriage plummeted with fewer desirable prospects. Hearing for the umpteenth time, "Don't worry, Mr. Right will come along" grew hollow. Certainly I still noticed the few men who came around, but I was also still bringing in my own groceries, mowing my own lawn, eating dinner alone, and going to church solo.

How quickly things can change when God decides the time is right! The week it all began for me was completely ordinary in the course of my work. I wasn't looking for love; in fact, I was emotionally burned out and "done" with relationships for a while. Yet love found me, right in my office where I was going about work as usual.

In *Sex and the Soul of a Woman*, Paula Rinehart writes, "In survey after survey, women insist that, while they value having more options in how they relate to men, they miss the sense of romance, of being pursued by a man."[1] Romance and the kind of adventurous pursuit I'd always dreamed of walked into my office that day. When I least expected it, I was about to discover a real relationship and God's unsurpassed faithfulness.

Whether you are single, married, divorced, or widowed, whether you are dating or have lost hope, if you are open to an engaging, inspiring, and witty story, you've found it. I pray it will draw you to the Source of all hope, to God Himself.

part 1

A Real-Life Love Story

Chapter 1

At First Glance

"Nice eyes, nice smile," I thought.

After my colleague Judie briefly introduced Randy to me near the drinking fountain outside my office, I quickly dismissed that thought, assuming Randy was married. But the next day, Judie smiled and poked me, beaming, "Randy is single!" My marvelous reply? "That's nice." Inside I rebuffed, *"Yeah, yeah. So what? I've been in situations like this many times before. A guy comes on the scene. I notice him. I start to like him. I wait. I hope. But nothing happens. God, I don't want to go through that again. Not right now."*

I felt like a wilted flower—physically exhausted after recently returning from five intense weeks in Russia, emotionally and mentally worn out from challenges at work, and spiritually drained on top of it all. Yet in spite of my depleted state, something inside me flickered faintly at Judie's words. Doesn't it feel good when someone thinks of you? Judie had thought of me. So, putting my protest aside, I prayed, *"OK, Lord, I guess if Judie took the time to think of me and introduce Randy, I'll be open if You want me to. I don't really want to, but at least I won't ignore him."*

Randy lived in Southern California and was visiting the headquarters of The Navigators, an international Christian missions organization where I worked. Retired several years from the Marines, Randy had just come on board with The Navigators full-time and had flown to Colorado Springs for a fundraising training seminar. Unbeknownst to him, I was part of the teaching team for that seminar.

Never married, I had just turned 39 and had questioned and hoped and wondered hundreds of times if God would ever bring me a wonderful, godly man. At this point in my life, hope was threadbare. Real was my experience of what Oswald Chambers describes as the patience of faith.

"Patience is more than endurance. A saint's life is in the hands of God like a bow and arrow in the hands of an archer. God is aiming at something the saint cannot see, and He stretches and strains, and every now and again the saint says—"I cannot stand any more." God does not heed, He goes on stretching till His purpose is in sight, then He lets fly. Trust yourself in God's hands. For what have you need of patience just now?"[2]

Chambers also points to the eternal truth that God is holy love. Therefore, we establish ourselves on that and fling ourselves in reckless confidence on God. The Lord was beautifully drawing me back to just that. After initially meeting Randy, and desperately wishing I could sit this one out, I surrendered to my professional duties and committed to do my best at the fundraising seminar. Randy's presence dimly registered on my frazzled radar. Funny how radar can change in seconds.

I wanted some indication of what Randy was like right away. If he turned out to be just another insincere charmer, I wanted no part of it. To observe more about Randy without him knowing, I walked into the large meeting room before the seminar started, looked around at the notebooks placed on each assigned chair, found the notebook with Randy's name on it, and switched it to a chair two seats over. I would be able to watch him better here. I would observe this man.

The day before our seminar started, I spontaneously sat in on another session taught to our new staff. Since this session was in the same building in which I worked, I wanted to evaluate its content. Guess who else was there?

After the session, I greeted the majority of new staff, including

Randy, and initiated small talk. "Thanks for coming." "Where are you from?" "How do you like Colorado Springs?" That part of my job I enjoyed, but I confess I remember little of that initial conversation with Randy. Randy, however, remembers it precisely, because that's when he learned where I grew up. I had no idea how significant that would be to him.

For the next five days, I focused on seminar responsibilities: Prepare for twenty-six new staff. Copy and assemble handouts. Set up the main meeting room. Participate in the meetings and events. Teach a few sessions. Coach a new staff. Interact and answer questions. Because I was focused on my work, Randy and I had little face-to-face interaction. Still, observation tells its own story.

I noticed Randy was thoughtful and a gentleman. He opened doors for people. He offered to help move chairs and arrange the meeting room. He greeted others politely and expressed genuine interest in them. He also organized a small group of new staff to visit one of the office staff in the hospital to cheer her up.

A few times I caught Randy glancing at me across the room. I smiled. I sensed he was observing me as well. He asked me business questions that I realized other people could have easily answered. After a couple of days Judie beamed at me again. "Sandy," she said, "He asked me if you were married!"

For one seminar lunch, I needed to drive my car over to the dining hall where meals were served. Randy lagged behind in the meeting room. So with a nervous flutter, I offered him a ride. As I turned the key in my Nissan's ignition that cold September day, the starter sputtered and refused to engage. I wanted to escape under my seat! Silently I pleaded, *"Please, Lord, let this car start. This is a terrible time for car problems!"* Turning the key again and again, I nervously chattered, "Oh, I've had trouble with this car all week . . . it should start if I keep trying . . . usually it starts."

Thankfully it finally did. During lunch, I asked Randy a few questions about the seminar. I noticed the thoughtfulness and quality of his responses.

On another day, we had free time after dinner. In a meeting room at the lodge where several staff stayed, Randy joined me and our friends Gene and Marilyn at a small table while others from our group played games and talked. Gene and Marilyn taught Randy to play a dice game called Farkle, which I already knew how to play. We all had fun and relaxed.

I noticed Randy's sense of humor and enjoyment of others. On the last day of the seminar, my team designed a fun closing celebration. We played a rousing game of laser tag and then celebrated with ice cream sundaes for everyone. Among all the tables at the restaurant, I searched for a spot boasting a good view of the whole group so I could emcee and give away zany prizes. Our coveted awards included squirt guns, a Frisbee, and a Nerf ball. A seat next to Randy happened to be free, so I asked if anyone was sitting there. He said no and offered the seat to me. The evening was about to get better.

During dessert, with no small fanfare, I distributed prizes while describing and applauding the individual accomplishments of the lucky winners. Then, following a public thank you to one and all, a spirited squirt gun fight broke out! After all the ruckus, everyone piled into cars and headed back to the conference center. On that short drive, two cars full of mature adults revealed an innate love of good ol'-fashioned fun. Randy and I were in separate cars. His driver expertly passed us while an accomplice suddenly threw water into our car window. So naturally at the next stoplight, I dashed out of our car and plastered silly putty on their windshield. The antics continued all the way home.

Back at the conference center—a 19th-century Tudor-style castle—we stepped out into another crisp, crystal-clear Colorado evening. All of us felt tired and happy to be done with the five-day seminar and mountain of hard work. Our friend and colleague Mike enthusiastically recruited a small band of us to a starry hike up to the bell tower on the castle rooftop, including Randy and me. Ten of us climbed up the castle's fire-escape ladder and tip-toed across a section of roof with a tiny flashlight and quiet chatter. One man lugged his guitar, and once on the roof, we spontaneously sang songs and hymns to our Lord. That unhurried and heartfelt worship was a taste of heaven! Tears filled my eyes in adoration of the Lord. I noticed that Randy sang some but stood off by himself about eight feet back from everyone else. He seemed subdued. I wanted to invite him to come closer and sit with the group, but I hesitated, feeling I didn't know him well enough to ask. Months later I discovered why he stayed quiet that night.

I sensed and observed Randy's interest and knew something had stirred between us. Awareness and attraction were evident, yet I hardly knew this man. The seminar ended the next morning, September 28, and all out-of-town staff had assigned rides to the airport. Would I get to say goodbye to him, I wondered? What would I say? What would he say? What if he didn't say anything? Would I ever hear from him again? I had to attend a meeting that morning, so I did not see Randy before he caught his ride to the airport. Later, after returning to my desk, a small, bright pink Post-It note immediately caught my eye. It read, *"Thanks for everything, Randy."* I tingled all over.

Unsure when or how, I knew I would hear from Randy again. An uncanny peace and excitement filled me, and I felt content to wait. Thankfully, I didn't have to wait long.

Chapter 2

Pursued

Completely worn out after the seminar, I rested a few days. I slept in, took a couple of leisurely walks, ate Chex cereal for supper, and watched "The Princess Bride." The next day, some time with the Lord sent a refreshing breeze to my depleted sail. And I found my mind wandering back to one man and the pink note he left. Did it mean I would hear from him again like I suspected, or was I setting myself up for disappointment? How long would I have to wait? I also wondered about all the things I didn't know about him. Had Randy been married before? Did he walk with God deeply? What was he really like? I knew so little about him. Was I nuts to be thinking about him so much?

The month before I met Randy, a summer "interest" had left me in tears. Participating in an intense summer missions trip to Russia was awesome. Don was on the team and had flirted with me during the five-week program. I liked Don and reciprocated. After returning to the U.S., I was eager to hear from him. Four weeks passed, but I heard nothing. Angry and hurt, I wrestled with God and my failure to live out Proverbs 4:23, "Watch over your heart with all diligence, for from it flow the springs of life." Why was I suckered too easily by a man's flirtations? On top of that, the previous fall, another man had also deceived me. I "circled the wagons" and resolved to keep better emotional distance next time.

After a few days of rest, on Monday I drove to the office for work. Checking my e-mail, my heart jumped when I saw a message from Randy. *"It's him!"* Such roller-coaster emotions! Only one month ago, I had steeled my resolve not to fall for any man's false charms, and now my heart skipped a beat at the sight of Randy's e-mail! Crazy? Fickle? Maybe, yet somehow this felt different. My wit kicked in gear in response to Randy's clever and engaging message. Longing but scared, I determined to take this one day at a time. I also decided to involve a few good friends in this "relationship." Without telling Randy, I forwarded a few friends copies of the messages Randy sent me. My friends were my "watchdogs." If they detected anything questionable or any "red flags" in his communication, they would sound the alarm.

I would later learn from Randy that after meeting me and then returning home to California, he definitely wanted to initiate with me. However, he hesitated. *"But Lord, I hardly know Sandy. I don't even know if she is dating anyone! What should I do? How do I proceed?"* After a long interaction with the Lord and His Word on the flight home, God gave Randy peace to trust Him, to take a risk and step out in faith, follow his heart, and make the first move. So Randy, a hunt-and-peck typist new to cyberspace and e-mail, ventured ahead and began his pursuit.

Subject: Thanks
Date: 9/29

Sandy,

Thanks for all your hard work, attention to detail, dedication, and looonngg hours at our fundraising seminar. It was extremely helpful for me and I'm motivated!

Pleasure meeting you and getting acquainted!

Choose from one of the following. Sandy:
Enjoys God
Is a Hoosier
Sings well

```
Is a prankster
Likes to laugh
Is a laser tag loser
Is a practical workshop leader
Is pretty good at Farkle (the dice game we played with
friends)
All of the above.
```

Thanks again!

Randy

Subject: Re: Thanks
Date: 10/2

Hello, Randy.

Thank you for your e-mail and the little Post-It note on my desk. I enjoyed it!

I am glad you were at the fundraising seminar. Trust it touched your life and gave you some good direction.

I have helped with many fundraising seminars and felt like the Lord made it good in spite of me this time. Mostly because I was only at about 40 percent of my normal capacity. I also remember our trek up to the castle bell tower and spontaneously singing songs unto our Lord and King. How absolutely blessed. I could have stayed and sung for hours.

By the way, here are the answers to last week's quiz:

Sandy was tired coming into the seminar, forgot her own name by the end, and slept until 10:00 the next morning.

She did not come into work on Friday and was allegedly found at the Baker Street Laser Quest.

Now here is this week's quiz:

Randy:
Is a potential candidate for Future Farkle Players of America
Is a gentleman
Can scale a castle by starlight with five chattering women, a few good men, a dinky flashlight, and no spinach
Needs a little work on his Nerf fast ball
Holds the record for singing "This Little Light of Mine" the most times
Passed the "Fundraising Navigation Obstacle Course"
After a so-so laser tag drill, ranked in the top two who won a free class: Laser Tag 101 for Marine Officers
All the above.

I appreciate your thoughtfulness and enjoyed getting to know you.

Sandy

Subject: Hello
Date: 10/2

Hello, Sandy.

You are humble, and it's a blessing to enjoy His in-spite-of-me love and care.

So now I feel shortchanged, by about 60 percent.

What does Sandy at 100 percent look like…bouncing off those laser tag walls or climbing castle steps to heaven? The castle bell tower time and singing were truly a fore-taste of the heavenly host at the feet of the Master.

Praise His lovely name!

Do all Navigator headquarters' staff have three-day weekends?

Even wearing name tags, only a Hoosier could forget her name at the end of the seminar. Ouch! There goes the me-being-a-gentleman bit.

All joking aside: When did you graduate from Ball State University? Did you become a Christian in college? Was it through Navigators?

Of course, you may disregard any comments or questions as you consider the source/author.

Just remember—I have Farkle potential, I have Farkle potential, I have Farkle potential….

Randy

P.S. I have to referee a high school boys' basketball game tonight.

Subject: Man with a whistle
Date: 10/4

Hello, Ref.

Moonlighting at the gym, huh? Was the basketball game a close one? Did you have to throw anybody out of the game?

As I mentioned, your last e-mail had me rolling. Appreciate it. And now in random order: At 100 percent, I am 100 percent. Ha! At 100 percent I am actually a professional singer, Fulbright scholar, guard for the

Springs' Vikings basketball team, blonde and five foot two.

My friends would definitely give a more accurate picture, but as my emotional tank fills up, I'm more extrovert and fun loving, enjoy relationships and hard work.

I'm also circulating a petition at headquarters to start three-day weekends more often, say once a month. This is an effort to make the Navigator staff administrative charge you pay get more bang for the buck. Your boss also voted for it.

Also, in reference to your clandestine question about my age, you have me beat by several gray hairs, but I graduated from Ball State University in 1982, then from the University of Colorado in 1993. These epic college years add up to a bachelors in marketing. Maybe someday I'll get the M (Masters) if I can do it debt free.

That sort of answers your question, but if you read on carefully, you might be able to decode the answer to how old I am.

God changed my life during college. Here's the cyberspace version, in less than 42 megabytes. Grew up a good girl, Catholic, always believed in God, Jesus, and the Bible. Did not really know the Bible, except for the more than 34 stories I heard for years during mass. Had a tender heart toward God, but had not heard of a personal relationship with Jesus Christ.

Grew up on a small pig farm, had good stability, hand-me-downs, and not much traveling because of not much money. So I was very naïve in just about everything when college came. My freshman year was tough, living off campus the first half, then in the dorm. There I met Vivian.

Vivian's life attracted me. She was friendly and open about God. Eventually she shared the gospel with me and I was ready. The next year I grew like a weed spiritually. Vivian was involved with Navigators, and that began the process of getting rooted in the Scriptures and surrendering all to Him. And I have always been fascinated with the Old Testament and how many books there are. I also helped out with all facets of the ministry and loved it. Those were hard years, but also some of the best.

I've been involved with Navigators ever since, through some good, bad, and ugly. And that is how the greatest decision of my life began, and there is nothing greater than knowing Him.

What about you, Major? How did the Lord get your attention and show Himself to you? Are you working full-time for Navigators, or do you work elsewhere too? Are you swashbuckling any more ships? Singing off any more castle rooftops?

By the way, you might want to skip Monday night football and instead practice Farkle. Next time you won't be given so many points. And as you practice, if you don't win against yourself, I know of a Farkle Anonymous 800 number.

Sandy

Subject: Random Order
Date: 10/5

Hello, Sandy, aka, Fuller Brush Scholar.

I refereed three games, had one over-time, two technical fouls and one ejection for hanging on the rim. All in a night's work. It gives me some fun, some money, some exercise, and pressure I enjoy.

Have you ever thought of high school volleyball refereeing?

Did you receive 2305 e-mail last night (11:05 PM for you

civilians and blondes)? I could not find it in my sent mail.

Your e-mails are hilarious—make my day! (Besides working on my fundraising, of course.)

Are you semi-pro or pro with the Vikings basketball? How long were you at 5' 2"? And speaking of blondes, how do you put a twinkle in a blonde's eye? Shine a flashlight in her ear.

I honor you for enjoying hard work. Me too! It's good medicine. Colossians 3:23.

I believe I have decoded you. Let me get this straight.

You attended a small college, Pig Farm State University in Colorado, and graduated in 1928 or 1939. You earned an epic Volleyball scholarship from some guy named Viking Fulbright. To fill your gas tank you were a professional guard and petition circulator. On your 3-day weekends, you marketed debt free bachelors for your boss and could be considered a Master. Nowadays, you prefer to refer to that clandestine activity with the decoded letter M. I don't blame you!

You are between 34 and 42 years old, but because of a tough freshman year, you don't remember. Things like that happen sometimes, even to good girls.

During that year you sustained 42 large, mega bites and sang 34 monotone songs. You taught the student population how to play Farkle and earned world-wide recognition for this feat. You are quite the amazing woman!

Thanks for sharing your conversion and growth in Christ. That's so neat!

My story to follow. For now, I must go practice Farkle.

Mr. Gray Hairs

Subject: Hello
Date: 10/6

Sandy,

Hello again and greetings in His grip! How are you feeling? How's that capacity tank?

Thanks again for sharing your spiritual journey. Exciting!

Thanks for asking about my story. I was born at a very early age…

I heard the gospel for the first time at a Young Life weekend retreat at Mt. Hermon, Santa Cruz, CA. I was attracted to the quality of life of the speaker, plus I was desperately looking for a purpose in life. God opened my eyes and understanding, and I prayed for the first time in my life and asked Christ to take over.

At age 16, God showed me 1) He knew me, 2) He accepted me in spite of me, and 3) Above all, He loved me. That changed me forever.

At that Young Life retreat, someone also gave me the Bridge to Life tract (which shares the gospel of Jesus Christ), and my introduction to The Navigators began. I wrote to The Navigators' address for Bible study.

I too met my first real-life Navigator as a college freshman. Don was a farmer who was helped by Navigators when he was in the Navy. He drove 45 minutes each way every Tuesday to meet with me in Bible study and to disciple me. He typed out some Bible verses for me and told me to memorize

them. I didn't know any better, so I did. That revolution-
ized my Christian life.

I went to conferences and spiritual-growth training pro-
grams, and God emblazed the passion and vision to exchange
my life for multiplying disciples. What an adventure! I
was involved with The Navigators' military ministry while
investing 20 years in the Marine Corps. So that makes 31
Navigator years, through some good, bad, and ugly. Even
excommunicated once.

As of August 1, I work full time on Navigator staff. I
also referee basketball for love of the game, a few dollars, fun, workout, and opportunities to serve and interact with others for the Lord.

With Navigators, I work with Sam and a team of four staff
couples in Southern California. For a more detailed explanation and history of God's grace in my life, I wrote a
12-page paper entitled "God's Call on My Life." If interested, it is yours upon request.

What's your Myers-Briggs type? Do you have any other
brothers and sisters besides a sister you mentioned?

Because He lives,

Randy

Subject: Order Random Order
Date: 10/6

Hi, Randy.

Now I know for sure. You have potential in the Creative Writing R Us
sweepstakes. What a kick! Thanks for both of your e-mails.

Today it has been work before relaxing, but it's been hard! The beautiful coating of snow this morning made me want to keep on driving up into the mountains for awhile. Almost did.

Congratulations on almost decoding the age question. Good start, but the exact answer of how old I am is still there.

I did receive your 11:05 e-mail. What are you doing checking your e-mail at 11:00 p.m.? And yes, I tried refereeing volleyball, a city park/recreation league. But I did not enjoy it as much as I thought I would. I knew that I would not get the referee of the year award!

Thanks too for sharing a bit of your testimony. I guess your sweet 16 really was sweet. And you were even later excommunicated—I'll have to hear that story sometime.

And you wrote a 12-page paper on the history of God's grace in your life. Wow. Did you not have an editor? Seriously, feel free to send it to me. It sounds interesting and insightful.

Thanks for asking how I'm feeling. I'm getting better, but it will take some more time to build my emotional reserves back up. It was a series of things over the past couple of months that took the wind out of my sail. But the sweetness of watching the Lord draw me back to His feet touches me deeply. The wonder of His voice and His love is so satisfying.

I'm headed out to dinner with some friends tonight. I look forward to a fire in the fireplace when I return. I'm also eager to start making Christmas wreaths this weekend. I make a few nice ones each year and sell them. This year the profits will help me be the maid of honor for one of my best friend's weddings. She is from St. Lucia in the Caribbean.

I also keep thinking of 2 Corinthians 5:21, "He made Him who knew no sin to be sin on our behalf, so that we might become the righteousness of God in Him." That is simply as amazing now as it was when I first met Him. How utterly compelling.

Be sure to visit Mt. Hermon again and be kind to all the farmers you know. Gotta go now and get some great Mexican food.

Sandy

Subject: Order Random Order Continued
Date: 10/6

Randy,

Believe it or not, I'm back in the office. I'm not a workaholic in the least, but had to come back stuffed with lasagna to get a paper a friend gave me today.

My Myers-Briggs type is ESFJ (Extrovert, Sensing, Feeling, Judgment), batting a 4.0 in the Feeling category.

And, by way of family...
I've never been married, but I have had 33-plus roommates, so that should count for something.
And I have enough siblings that you can borrow a couple if you'd like.
4 brothers, 3 sisters
I am #5
17 nieces and nephews with another one on the way
15 Farkle dice
6 decks of cards

In my family, I am the one who is "away," which is God's fault. I often miss my family, but I'm grateful for all the Lord has taught me in the process.

One new Farkle rule I discovered this week: On your seventh roll of the dice, you must close your eyes, then randomly pick which die you want to keep.

Hope you are spending your few dollars, tracking all your Bridges, coding your decoder, emblazing some Tuesday conferences, hanging on the rim of those slippery e-mails, and exchanging some 12-pagers.

Sweet dreams.

Sandy

Subject: Hostess of the World
Date: 10/7

Hello, Sweet Dreams.

The town I live in is Fallbrook, the avocado capitol of the world. A little guacamole and salsa hit the spot!

Okay - you are less than 42 years old but more than 34, so that means you are 39 because you are fascinated with the number of Old Testament books. When is the BIG 40? Have you ever thought of writing mysteries?

I sent you my 12 page paper in mail today.

Also, the last four months I have had a Bible study on the base at Camp Pendleton. Good news...three Marines have trusted Christ as their Savior!

If you were to write a book, what would the subject be? I think mine would be: The God-dependent Life.

You being an ESFJ on the Myers-Briggs—"Hostess of the World"—explains your 33-plus roommates. An ESFJ is gracious, good interpersonal skills, thoughtful, appropriate, eager to please, most harmonizing.

I am an ISFJ—"A High Sense of Duty." An ISFJ is amiable,

works behind the scenes, ready to sacrifice, accountable, prefers doing. Most loyal.

If I may be so bold, why haven't you married?

Is your family in Indiana? My folks and family live in the San Francisco Bay area except for one brother who is a professor at the Univ of South Carolina. I have three brothers, one sister. I am number two—must be where loyal characteristic comes from.

I hope your emotional reserves will be built back up with beautiful snow, cozy fires, good friends, Holy Spirit comfort, and nuggets from His precious Word!!

Randy

Subject: Three Cheers
Date: 10/9

Hello, Randy.

Thanks for your e-mails. And congratulations on figuring out my age, 39. The big 40 comes next August for me, but I'm trying to not think about it.

Three cheers for the three Marines who have trusted Christ!

Thanks too for your question on what book would I write. These are a few ideas for magazine articles:
Importance of short-term missions
Why many Christian singles don't go to church
Something on praying
Something for women on: speak up!

If it were a book . . . need to think on that. I might write a short version on the journey to intimacy with God.

Regarding your other question about why I haven't married, I need to think for a bit first.

I guess you having boldness comes from a High Sense of Duty, or from being on the ship deck for several years. But I don't mind. I have a degree of the same.

Cheers to doing, and to being. For the One who is worthy.

Sandy

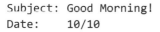

Subject: Good Morning!
Date: 10/10

Sandy,

No, congrats to you on number 39!

I also see the supreme value of short-term missions. My military experience transferred me every three years to a different three-year mission (duty station). That's similar to short-term missions.

Your topic of why single Christians don't go to church is interesting. I've experienced the church doing more harm than good with this neglected, large population (all ages). It is a key need of the hour and a key ministry opportunity. Publish or perish. You will be read!

Question: Did Eve ever have a date with Adam?

I've been thinking about Job. The Lord believed him to be

faithful enough to allow his suffering. Despite the terrible pain, Job did not believe the Lord was unjust. If I claim to belong to Him, then everything I possess and love, outwardly and inwardly, is His.

"My goal is God Himself, not joy, nor peace, nor even blessing, but Himself, my God." -Oswald Chambers.

Answer: No, it was an apple.

Randy

Subject: Chambers salute
Date: 10/10

Dear Randy,

To an Oswald Chambers fan. I love Oswald Chambers and could not have said it better.

Yep, all of my immediate family live in Indiana, most within two hours of each other. They are surrounded by majestic corn fields and bean fields.

Now for the question that made me think a while—why I have never married. I've been asked that several times, but how to answer it depends. I shall answer it if you agree to answer the parallel question, why are you not married? Drink some guacamole tea while you consider that one.

And so, to answer why I never married. Because:

I have not been asked.
I have not found the right one.
I did not want to marry just to be married.

One man I wanted to ask me didn't.
For many years in my twenties, I did not like men, nor
Think I wanted them. Nor was I ready.
I have been too picky at times.
I have not been picky enough sometimes.
I have not found many men passionate about God.

But the truth is, I don't know.
I don't see it so much as by my choice,
But it's a mystery.
It is not for a lack of want.
But if it comes,
I do not want it to be just for fear of being alone at 60,
But for love and life and His goodness.

Hope you are having a good afternoon (that's civilian for after AM
turns to PM).

Sandy

Subject: Sharing
Date: 10/10

Sandy,

Thanks for sharing, being transparent, and vulnerable.
You're great!

Devotionally, I really enjoy Mrs. Charles Cowman in her
book "Streams in the Desert."

Question: Do I believe in love?

In June 1999 I went on a weeklong basketball boondoggle
(fun trip) through Hoosierland. One of my favorite movies

was "Hoosiers." Have you seen it? I followed the bouncing basketball through Indianapolis, New Castle, French Lick, Knightstown, Milan, and more. (Milan is the real 1954 state champs which the movie is based on. I also met the real star of the game, Bobby Plump.) I have fond memories, met super people, and have great Indiana stories to tell. God opened some amazing doors and provided to the detail.

I gladly agree to answer the parallel question of why I am not married, in a little while. First, I'd like you to read my 12-page documentary. It will give you some helpful background information. Please let me know when you receive it. In the meantime, one reason is because of the warning in Ecclesiastes 7:26.

Another reason—suffice it to say that God has not brought a companion into my life who would wholeheartedly embrace my personal philosophy for life and ministry. That is: to know, love, and glorify God, and to be used of Him to raise up qualified laborers in significant numbers as fast as possible to help fulfill the Great Commission.

As I'm sure your heart cries out, it's gotta be a God thing. After all, He created marriage—Genesis 2:22.

I'm also a firm believer in "God's will done in God's way in God's time will not lack God's support."

Answer: I believe in love because I believe in God, and God is love.

What qualities are you looking for in a mate?

Because of His great passion,

Randy

Chapter 3

Full Disclosure

After only two weeks of correspondence like this, I was fast becoming hooked on Randy. Like a yo-yo, I bounced from, *"Am I crazy? Why am I letting myself fall for this man whom I know so little about?"* to, *"This is so exciting!"*

When Randy asked about the qualities I was looking for in a mate, I thought, *"This guy doesn't waste any time!"* Normally I would have been turned off by such a question. It's too forward and awkward to answer. Before rattling off my list, I wanted to see if this man had some of the qualities on it already. Otherwise, he could try to become what he thought I wanted him to be just to win me over. Certainly that might feel good. It's also loaded with potential for a hilarious movie script, but it is not real. So, how would I answer Randy's question?

After my two recent experiences with men who had deceived me, my push-pull emotional circus raged on. *"Yes, I like Randy . . . this is amazing . . . he is different. Lord, are You doing something here? Could he be The One?"* Then the other side would kick in. *"Watch out for those false charmers. You don't know him that well."* My ideal had always been to spend lots of time around the man I liked to observe him, discern his character and his heart for God, and let my friends get to know him. I cried out to God, *"You have to help me with this! How can I observe Randy when he lives in California? Lord, please show me. This is not the way I thought it would be."*

Despite the persistent tug-of-war, I felt something resurrected in me, something good and long awaited. It was my hope for real relationship. I'll never forget my exhilaration after my friend Susie read two weeks of e-mails between Randy and me and exclaimed, "Oh my gosh, Sandy, this is real!"

Beyond the E-mails

I appreciated that Randy, always goal-oriented, was owning his interest in me and pursuing me. This was something pretty foreign to me. In addition to e-mailing, he sent a few thoughtful items that showed up in my mailbox. Inside one manila envelope was a hand-made collage of flower cut-outs, get-well wishes, stickers, and funny pictures. I smiled and tingled and cried. Randy remembered how exhausted I felt and sought to cheer me up. That spoke volumes. He was thinking of me!

I also received a card from Randy in which he included a check made out to me with a note: "Please use this money to fix your car—I think your starter needs replaced." Not only had Randy been thoughtful enough to remember my car problems, but he was willing to help pay to fix them! No one had ever paid for my car repair before, and I felt completely at peace with it.

Feeling dog-tired and needing encouragement, I accepted his thoughtfulness and gifts and simply enjoyed it all. Interestingly, Randy later told me that on the day he heard my faulty starter, he thought, *"I like this girl and there is a need here. I want to help out."*

Another manila envelope from Randy arrived. Inside was a twelve-page paper detailing God's grace in Randy's life and outlining how God had led and called him to minister over the years. More tears came as I realized Randy's willingness and invitation to let me read his paper—a glimpse into his heart and life. The pages revealed Randy's deep love for and commitment to God.

With this paper, he included a short note telling me that he had three daughters, and that several years ago his former wife had divorced him. Later I learned that not only had she committed adultery and left their marriage, but unbelievably she had abandoned their children as well. Instantly, I grieved for the tragedy and enormous heartache

Randy and his girls had experienced.

This was the first time I had heard that Randy was divorced and had children. Part of me felt disappointed because I did not necessarily want to marry someone who was divorced. At my age, and with an unfortunately high divorce rate for even Christians, I realized it was a possibility. Yet I secretly hoped that there might be a never-married man or a widower out there somewhere for me. Since I had waited all this time and stayed a virgin, surely God could honor me in that way. For a while, I had to work through various feelings about Randy being divorced. Later on, the Holy Spirit prodded me. If the Lord Himself had chosen a great man for me, and he happened to be divorced, who was I to say no? Who was I to dictate to God? As I surrendered and accepted what God may have ordained, peace followed.

Immediately, while hurting for the pain Randy and his girls had endured, I knew two things. First, at the right time, I wanted to hear the details about what happened, why the divorce, and how things stood now. This would help determine if Randy was someone I could marry or not. I had met too many divorced men with significant character issues that came as a result of broken marriages. Some were bitter, some were not fully recovered, while others seemed to have learned little from their pain.

Second, I realized that divorce was not a deal-breaker. Years ago I had studied the Sermon on the Mount in Matthew, and chapter five includes divorce. Jesus blasted the religious leaders for their selfish and ridiculous justifications for divorce. Clearly, God hates divorce. However, He allows it in certain instances like adultery. It is important to look at each situation individually. God can restore. He can make new.

I also wondered what Randy's grown daughters were like. What did they think of my relationship with their dad? What would they think of me? How could I get to know them when I lived so far away? Would they let me be a part of their lives? I hoped so. If they did not accept me or let me into their lives, I wouldn't know how to handle it.

But I also found that I had already accepted them, without even meeting them! I accepted them just because they were Randy's daughters.

A few years later, Randy told me he felt nervous, hesitant, and somewhat scared to tell me he was divorced. That, and being a single parent, was a truckload to tell me all at once. He worried that I might have a stigma against divorcees and would break it off before we even got fully started.

By the time he met me, Randy had been a single parent for just over nine years after his former wife had deserted the family and later divorced Randy. For most of that time, he focused on raising his daughters alone, finished out the last years of his career in the Marines, and then worked several jobs after that. He also never sensed the freedom from the Lord to look for a new wife. But when God chose to bless him with that freedom, it came in a way that was powerful, unmistakable, and designed especially with Randy in mind.

Chapter 4

Prepared

The week we met, Randy's state of mind and heart were the opposite of mine. I was emotionally, mentally, physically, and spiritually exhausted, and therefore not interested in "checking out" any single men. But for Randy, it was different. God had primed and prepared his heart.

This is Randy's story, in his own words.

In 1991, my life turned upside down when I became a single parent raising three daughters, ages 10, 12, and 15 for the next ten years. My former wife had betrayed me, abandoned me and our children, never repented, and later divorced me. I was still an active-duty Marine Corps infantry officer for three of those ten years, completing a twenty-year military career. At that time, little could I imagine what God was orchestrating on my behalf.

During those initial, difficult years of just me and the girls, Dan, a longtime friend and mentor, came to see me and also talked with me on the phone several times. One of his most memorable visits came five years after my former wife had left. Dan again took time from his international ministry to come visit me and my daughters in my small apartment in Fallbrook, California. I can't tell you how much that meant. Dan shared his heart and love with me, as he had for many years. Then he told me something I have never forgotten. It was so poignant that I wrote in my Bible, "Dan's Visit, April 30," next to the verse he shared with me.

God had spoken to Dan's heart as he thought about and prayed for me and my future. Dan gave me Job 8:19–20 (NASB) as God's encouragement and promise for me personally:

"Behold, this is the joy of His way;

And out of the dust others will spring.

Lo, God will not reject a man of integrity,

Nor will He support the evildoers."

I cried. God affirmed His amazing love to me and told me that though things were hard now, a day would come when things would be different! God was still my chief joy. He never rejected me. I felt comforted, loved, guided, and encouraged that day and many days following.

As Dan shared that promise from Job, the word "behold" did not stand out in any particular way. God affirmed and confirmed that I was obeying Him in my heart even after five tough years of single parenting following a divorce. For me at that time, this was "the joy of His way."

I also wondered if the words "out of the dust others will spring" could mean the Lord would bring along a wife in my future. Only time would tell. What I knew for sure was that God's standard of holiness and integrity was personally affirmed to me. I was not forgotten! Nor shelved. God still had marvelous plans and purposes for me. His loving presence and hope infused me. Though God hates divorce (Malachi 3:10), He incredibly loves divorcees! Jeremiah 31:3 (NASB) proclaims, "I [the LORD] have loved you with an everlasting love; therefore I have drawn you with lovingkindness."

Dan's visit proved a divine appointment from a sovereign and loving Lord. God had mercy on me. Dan became God's messenger to a lonely and emotionally broken man. Through those difficult years, I continued to discover that walking in God's ways and striving to be a man of integrity for Jesus Christ would result in joy worth beholding.

A year after Dan's visit, I decided to take a sorely needed, one-week dream vacation. For this basketball enthusiast, that meant several days in basketball heaven—Indiana, Hoosierland, where basketball is king! During this basketball boondoggle (a loosely scheduled, fun trip), my one focus was to enjoy the sights, folklore, history, and people of this basketball-crazed region. I had no idea the surprise God would give me there.

In the small town of French Lick, I played basketball on Larry Bird's home court and met his brother. I visited the Indiana Basketball Hall of Fame and walked inside the largest high school gym in the world in New Castle. I spent a night at the Steve Alford Hotel and felt privileged to get my picture taken with Bobby Plump (star of the 1954 state-champion Milan basketball team, upon which the movie "Hoosiers" is based).

Toward the end, I cruised past endless rows of cornfields when, out of the blue, the Holy Spirit spoke to my heart as only God can do. Though not audible, His Spirit communicated to my spirit, saying, "What would you think if I brought a woman from Indiana into your life to be your wife?"

Dumbfounded, I wondered where that came from. I knew no one from Indiana! Strange indeed. My trip ended, and I flew back home to California. Over the following days and weeks, I tucked it away in the recesses of my heart. After nothing much happened, it faded.

Fast forward three years. For fun and encouragement, I attended an old-timers' Navigator reunion in Colorado Springs. Missionary Roy Robertson shared a memory about how Navigator founder Dawson Trotman prayed for him as Roy, the first Navigator overseas missionary, was being sent to China. After praying, Dawson gave Roy a promise from Isaiah 43:19 (NASB): "Behold, I will do something new, Now it will spring forth; Will you not be aware of it? I will even make a roadway in the wilderness, rivers in the desert."

The conference ended and I flew home to California, blessed by Roy and so many dear saints of God. Twenty-one days after hearing Isaiah 43:19 in Colorado, a small card arrived in my mailbox from friends. After signing it, guess what they wrote at the bottom? Isaiah 43:19.

Twelve days later I flew to Colorado Springs again for a ten-day training and orientation seminar for new Navigator staff. During those days, every time I started to review some Scripture memory verses, I could get no further than Job 8:19–20. Those words Dan had shared with me years ago kept echoing over and over in my mind. It was like an arrow piercing my heart, and I could not shake it off. God was brewing something.

During this conference, I met Sandy. After one of our early meetings, aiming to be polite and sociable, I asked Sandy where she was from. When she answered, "Indiana," I about fell over! I mumbled something and excused myself.

I did not see Sandy again until two days later. I was instantly attracted to her character, poise, and spirit. Even though we were not able to talk much during the seminar, I observed her like a hawk. Launching a clandestine operation, I asked a few people who knew Sandy some basic questions about her. Out of the blue during lunch, I asked Sandy's colleague, Judie, "Is Sandy married?" Judie replied, "No, but I think she would like to be."

After four or five days observing Sandy, the seminar concluded, and I ended up joining a small group of people who trekked up to the bell tower atop Glen Eyrie's castle. Sandy came too. This group spontaneously sang songs of worship to our Lord Jesus Christ. I stood back and observed Sandy worshiping the Lord from a genuine heart. I witnessed her heart and love for the Savior. Overwhelmed and crying, I could not sing. We worshiped our great God with beautiful music on a spectacular moonlit evening. I was overcome by God, by this small group of missionaries surrendering all to Him, by everything! That night I knew I had fallen in love with Sandy.

Yet I barely knew her! I didn't even know if she was dating anyone. The next morning before leaving for the airport, I did not see Sandy, but I left her a note on her desk.

On the plane ride back to California, I struggled with what God was obviously doing in my heart regarding Sandy and the two "behold" verses (Job 8:19–20 and Isaiah 43:19). What was I supposed to do now? After I surrendered to the Holy Spirit, He led me to diligently seek Him and journal my thoughts for thirty days.

As the Lord gave me grace to be obedient to journaling, He beautifully blended Job 8 and Isaiah 43. Job 8 promises that "others will spring," and Isaiah 43 says "now it will spring forth." Both verses begin with "behold," so I knew I needed to "behold" God speaking to me. He was doing something new. My thoughts raced, "When will it spring forth? How? Will I even be aware of it?" But God said He would "make a roadway in the wilderness and rivers in the desert." In other words, it would be very clear!

"God, what about my three daughters? How will they react? Are they ready for a stepmother?" I wondered. God's Spirit comforted me with His peace, rest, and quietness. He would take care of this too. Isaiah 32:17 (KJV) says, "And the work of righteousness shall be peace; and the effect of righteousness, quietness and assurance forever."

When I arrived home, my two daughters who still lived there greeted me at separate times. Amazingly, both asked the same question, "So, what's her name?" Stunned, I wondered how they could possibly know that I believed I'd found my future wife.

Only one answer was possible. God had prepared their hearts by telling Mirachelle and Merrilee individually.

All the while I was e-mailing and getting to know Sandy, I kept seeking God and journaling thoughts, questions, and things I was learning from His Word. I yielded to the Lord and wanted God to give me His confirmation and leading to pursue this relationship. During and after those thirty days, God clearly spoke to me and confirmed through His Word to continue pursuing this relationship with Sandy. I felt overjoyed! Precisely one day after those thirty days ended, I listened to an old message by Lila Trotman, wife of Navigator founder Dawson Trotman. She used Isaiah 43:19! The Holy Spirit bore witness with my spirit that once again, as the Lord promised, He made His ways clear.

In talking with a few trusted people who knew Sandy, here is what I heard:

"She is strong in the Lord."

"She is lively, creative, fun."

"Sandy has a heart for overseas and is a hard worker."

"I never could figure out why she was single. There are lots of blind men around."

"Sandy is a wonderful woman, and I am always amazed at how deep and talented she is."

"She is the best listener I have ever met."

"We regard Sandy as one of the great women we know."

In addition, one dear couple prayed for a godly woman for me every day during a season before I met Sandy. They stuck notes all around their house as prayer reminders. What a blessing!

God indeed made it clear. Everything pointed to "Yes!" All the lights showed green (go for it), and none were yellow or red (caution or stop). I was in love with Sandy, and I knew God orchestrated it all. Ecstatic, I knew Sandy was the one for me! Now I just needed to get to know her!

Defining the Relationship

With Randy's heart prepared and in full pursuit, he clarified his intentions to me through his e-mail messages. By taking the initiative to define the relationship, it spoke volumes of his respect and integrity, and it created freedom and safety to allow him a bigger place in my heart and life. Now we could continue getting to know one another better with the purpose of seeing if God might lead us to marry. In the past, defining the relationship was a critical piece missing from most of my relationships with men; I erred in giving my heart away anyway. I paid the price with heartache.

This time was different. Randy's integrity launched a new song in my heart.

Subject: Hello
Date: 10/11

Hi Randy.

Can't talk long as I'm headed into a half-day meeting soon.

I received both of your manila envelopes yesterday. THANK YOU! Absolutely loved the "get well" collage! It made me cry and laugh and cry and...

You are hilarious. Thanks too for your 12-page calling paper and the snapshot of your life then and now. I read it. Wow. There is much in there with your heart and a big part of your life. I appreciate your willingness to share it with me. I am so sorry to hear about what happened with your former wife's unfaithfulness and that she completely abandoned the family. My heart ached for you and your girls.

Last night I read, "Do not let your heart be troubled. Believe in God, believe also in Me. In my Father's house are many rooms...I am going there to prepare a place for you...and I will come back and take you to be with Me."

Be encouraged. That is our destiny.

Sandy

Subject: Destiny
Date: 10/11

Sandy,

Hope your meeting was encouraging and productive! Some meetings are and some are not.

I am glad you enjoyed the collage—trust it helps you restore your reservoir!

Thanks for taking the time to read my calling paper and your encouragement.

Just this morning I read in *Streams in the Desert*:

"Measure thy life by loss and not by gain,
Not by the wine drunk, but by the wine poured forth.
For love's strength standeth in love's sacrifice.
And he who suffers most has most to give."

Thanks for sharing from John 14—very encouraging. It's especially comforting to know that He reigns supreme and prepares a special place for each of His children . . . a destiny.

I can't figure out your mail system. I mailed a card to
you last Wednesday, the collage on Friday, and the paper
on Saturday. Interesting that the Heavenly Mail Carrier
delivered the collage and paper the same day! Any sign of
the card?

When we really come down to the bottom line of life, if we
are truly honest, wouldn't you agree that it is as simple
as "crying and laughing and crying and laughing," before
the Master, and before God-given men and women? That too
is destiny.

God is so Good.

Randy

Subject: You've Got Mail
Date: 10/11

Hi, Randy.

Yes, since more Californians are moving to Colorado each year, they
amended the mail delivery system to specifically thwart the influx.
They advertised with: Mail Any Day...Delivery Any Day After.

Yes, I received your card, which also made me smile and cry. That was
generous of you and very sweet. I sent you a thank you in the mail on
Monday.

The meeting this morning—Have you heard of Leadership Catalyst and
Bill Thrall? He's co-authored a book called *The Ascent of a Leader*. We
have been required to attend four sessions of this training. It deals
with character as central to leadership. Everyone's a leader. Leaders grow in environments of grace. Some of the content is good and
supposed to be worked out on our teams. Our team has had major

difficulties the past month, which has made it interesting.

So, you've been a Hoosier at heart for awhile. Yes, I like the movie Hoosiers. My dad actually remembers the real game and told me a little about it. The ending minutes of the game were actually a stall.

Ecclesiastes 7:26, the verse you mentioned about why you are not married. Hum, I can see why it was left out of the Topical Memory System of verses to memorize.

And for the question of the decade: What qualities am I looking for in a mate? Suffice it to say: One who loves the Lord with all his heart, mind and strength.

I think for Hoosiers II, they might be looking for a good referee. And you won't have to go to any unproductive town meetings.

But the real question is: What did you think about Indiana University firing Bobby Knight? Was it destiny?

Sandy

Subject: You've Got Spunk
Date: 10/12

Hello, Hoosier.

I think the firing of Bobby Knight was long overdue. He believed he was above the law and untouchable. My coaching hero of any sport has to be John Wooden from UCLA. His roots are Martinsville, then Purdue University.

I've e-mailed Knight and invited him to attend your Leadership Catalyst classes. Maybe Bill Thrall can write the *Descent of a Leader* with Bobby.

No, I haven't heard of Thrall, but I agree leadership apart from character is substandard. Everyone's a leader because everyone influences—for good or bad, and leaders grow in environments of grace. We need the freedom to fail or we won't take risks of faith.

Would you believe I have a copy of the real Hoosiers 1954 game won by Milan? You are 100 percent correct—the last few minutes was a stall.

Where in Indiana do you hail from?

I promised you an answer about why I haven't married after you read my 12-page calling paper. For the last 10 years I have been mom and dad, worked several jobs, and done ministry. Either out of no time or little desire, I wasn't looking. Within the last year, God has restored that desire and given me some precious promises.

The real question of the century is: What is Sandy going to be for Halloween?

Randy

Subject: You've Got Connections
Date: 10/13

Hey, Coach.

You have a copy of the real '54 Milan championship game, and an autograph of John Wooden, coach par excellence…. I am impressed. You've got connections and clout and class. I would love to see the real Milan game sometime.

And I totally agree about Bobby Knight. They should have fired him years ago. Talent is one thing, how you play is another. We used to call that sportsmanship.

If Bobby Knight comes to our Leadership Catalyst seminar, you have to come as well to be our security.

I am from a town probably much like Milan, only in the opposite quadrant. The town is Reynolds, where the highlight is still watching the traffic go by at the only stoplight. It's about 30 minutes north of Lafayette/Purdue country.

Today I have taken the day off to do something the Lord has directed me to do. I wanted to spend some time with Him and look back over some journals to pick out lessons and important points of the last four to five years. Not sure what all will come of it, but I think it may be part of some new leading somehow.

You mentioned you have been mom and dad to your daughters for the past 10 years. That's pretty incredible and I respect that. You certainly have been through more in 10 years than many people. No doubt you could write another 12-page paper or book on what God has done for you and for your girls. May He keep on doing good things for you, whether from the path of suffering and healing, or the path of the living water of life and pastures of green.

Also, you asked for my comments about your calling paper. I have thought about it. What are you thinking in terms of what mode of feedback? Do basketball coaches and Hoosier fans and Wooden wanna-be's use their telephones much?

What will I be for Halloween, now that is a good question—maybe a pair of dice in salute to Farkle.

Don't stay out too late reffing tonight. Unless of course there is a long stall at the end of the game and the fans come wildly out of the stands in celebration. Rumor has it that they are asking for autographs from refs now, even in Fallbrook.

Sandy

Subject: Classy Woman
Date: 10/14

Dear Classy Woman,

Thank you for being you! You're the Class Act!

Thanks for taking the time to communicate and share
yourself through e-mail. I really look forward to your
communiqués!

How was your time alone with God? Would you care to share
any leading you received?

Thanks for your respect and perspective on my single parenting efforts. Madame Guyon, author of *Experiencing the
Depths of Jesus Christ,* once remarked, "I have learnt to
love the darkness of sorrow; there you see the brightness
of His face."

Along these lines, I have been motivated over the years
with the promise of Genesis 50:19-21.

Thanks for being so faithful with my questions—you don't
miss a beat! Regarding your question on what type of feedback I was looking for from my calling paper—I just wanted
to share some of my past and be up front, honest, transparent and straightforward with you. You deserve that.

I feel very comfortable in my interest in you and I
believe the Lord is leading me to develop this friendship.

If this is not how God is currently leading you, or if
there are some concerns, please feel free to express them.

In no way do I want to mislead or defraud you.

Your Halloween surprise was mailed on Friday so you may receive it by Halloween. Are you scared?

Randy

Chapter 5

Real Relationship at Last

Elated, my heart raced while reading Randy's words at least twenty-five times: "I feel very comfortable in my interest in you, and I believe the Lord is leading me to develop this friendship." This was real! A dam burst in my heart as Randy stated his intentions. It was one delicious moment, and I could hardly sleep for a week!

Coming back to earth briefly, I wrote my response, "Yes, yes, yes!!" Well, not really. That's what I wanted to say, but I figured that was too electric and too soon. So instead I said, "What God has done through you these past few weeks has been special and a wonderful gift to me. Thanks for your honesty, for letting me in on part of your life, and for taking a chance. I very much enjoy hearing from you! I love your sense of humor, your openness, and your heart. And I am comfortable too in my interest in you and moving ahead with our friendship. Of course there are questions and concerns, and we can deal with them along the way."

I already knew. In my soul I sensed God was in this, and that this was it, the real thing! Could it really be after the hundreds of times of waiting and wanting and praying? Could this man be as great as he seemed? No question I was falling for Randy, but I still had a little homework to do. Knowing next to nothing about the military, I scrambled to find a crash course. I asked a friend who had been a military spouse to tell me exactly what it was that Marines did. Semper Fi (always faithful) entered my vocabulary. "First to strike on air, land, and sea" took on new meaning, as well as "on duty 24/7."

I was also learning more about Randy's heart. Proverbs 27:19 says,

"As water reflects a face, so a man's heart reflects the man." Among some of the positive things I learned:

- ✓ Randy and I both had a heart for missions.
- ✓ Randy genuinely cared about my friends, which meant a lot to me.
- ✓ We were attracted to one another's sense of humor. He mailed me a box for Halloween and said to be careful opening it. Inside was a fake left arm along with a funny poem.
- ✓ Randy was responsive. After a few weeks of e-mails, there came a time when I thought some things were easier to talk about rather than e-mail. After I gave him a subtle hint to "feel free to call if you'd like," Randy asked, "When is a good time to call you?"
- ✓ Randy's character and life were molded and shaped through suffering too, and I respected that. It drew me to his heart.
- ✓ We could relate to similar life lessons. After sharing that I should have confronted someone much sooner than I did in a relationship, Randy understood.

These things drew our hearts together in respect and admiration. Randy's daughters "required" him to read Elisabeth Elliot's book, *Quest for Love*. I also bought a copy, read it, and later discussed it with Randy.

Just a week or two after our e-mails were in full swing, Randy started calling me. Relating to each other on a different level now, these calls made Randy want to see me again in person. During one of our phone calls, I remember chuckling when he blurted out, "Why don't you come out to California for a visit? You could also get some rest and relaxation too." Because I was frustrated with my job and still rebuilding my emotional reserves, this thoughtful man offered a chance for me to get away for a while. He also wanted to see me!

Thanking him for the offer, I said I would let him know.

Of course I wanted to visit Randy, but my yo-yo brain countered, "Is it proper to let a man pay for my way to come out and visit him? Is it too soon? Too forward? Just days earlier, my spiritual mentor had advised, "Sandy, you need to think about going out to see Randy, maybe sometime this fall." A little slow on the draw, I thought, "Oh yeah, you're right. I should think about that." Another friend concluded that I needed some in-person time with Randy. With that, I was assured and told Randy the next day that yes, I would come!

Subject: Tentative Itinerary
Date: 10/21

Sandy,

Here's a tentative itinerary for when you come to visit.

Day 1:
10:30   Arrival
12:30   Arrival if flying United
1:00   Customs, immunizations, and quarantine for Hoo-
         siers entering California
1:30   Complete lost luggage paperwork
2:00   Arrival serenaded by Marine Corps Drum and Bugle
         Corps
2:30   Try to locate car in airport parking lot
3:00   Take a break and review rule changes in upcoming
         basketball season
3:30   Find my car and replace the starter
4:00   Quick stop at Salvation Army for temporary cloth-
         ing issue
4:30   Shop for a hand (either right or left)
5:00   Visit San Diego Sea World and feed sharks, pet
         dolphins, and ride Shamu
5:30   Drive to LaJolla Cove and spear fish for dinner

```
6:00     Open all the gates at the Wild Animal Park
6:30     Walk Seaport Village and sell Navigator T-shirts
7:00     Take Trolley to Tijuana for tacos on T-shirt
         profits
7:30     Return to Fallbrook for Farkle and guacamole
8:00     Watch the 1954 Milan Championship Game
10:00    Fast and pray over your decision-making ability
         to ever get involved with men
12:00    Try to sleep
4:30     AM volleyball practice
```

Sincerely,

Lefty

Subject: Adjustments
Date: 10/23

Dear Lefty Randy,

The Colorado staff have voted and squeaked out an approval for your submitted trip itinerary for my visit, with the following adjustments:

* Have some seaweed soup in LaJolla
* Rent two camels from the Wild Animal Park for airport pick up
* Do a combo taco, T-shirt and tattoo party
* Check out Tijuana's Farkle Accessories Unlimited near the Hyatt Regency
* Find out if there really is a Montezuma, and where it is
* Drop and give 50 push-ups during the Bugle Corps
* Add a 6 AM Monday meeting and have a truly Quiet Time Devotional
* Pray and fast, or pray fast over my new book, *Some Men are From Mars, Many are From Pluto*
* Sing the Marine Corps song

I'm sleepy this morning but doing well.

Have to go and make a stop at home and make sure the window man is really installing new windows at my house. Never thought I would get excited about new windows, but then again, the air is thin in Colorado.

Sandy

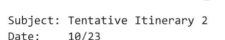

Subject: Tentative Itinerary 2
Date: 10/23

Good Morning, Trained Professional,

Thanks for sending me the great surprise, Toy Story 2! I will watch it soon. And seriously, here is tentative itinerary two for your time here:

Friday: One-hour Harbor Cruise, walk Seaport Village, dinner with Sam and Shirley in downtown San Diego's Gas Lamp Quarter

Saturday: Oceanside Pier, Beach, Boardwalk, Fallbrook, Church, dinner at Claim Jumper

Sunday: Trip to Catalina Island

Monday: San Diego Old Town, Marine Recruit Depot

Woman, there is no such thing as the Marine Corps song, but I did do my best to sing the Marine Corps Hymn prior to opening the classified said package.

As you requested, the above itinerary will be adjusted to reflect the following:
6,000 seaweed Tacos

90 sleeping camels
50 two-minute tattoos

Also, I would be curious to know when you "sensed my interest in you."

Sincerely,

Pluto Montezuma
Customer Service Specialist

Subject: Thanks
Date: 10/24

Hey, Pluto Randy, thanks for your letter. I'll be in touch.

And while it may be true that the Marine Corps does not have a song, we civilians know that the real answer is: The Marine Corps does not have a song, yet. I've heard they can be a little resistant to change.

CTP
(Civilian Trained Professional)

Subject: Good Morning
Date: 10/25

Sandy,

Good morning from the Sunshine State! This is going to be a good day because of the Lord Jesus Christ, but also because I'm going to try to view the movie you sent me, Toy Story 2!

On Monday, October 23 I read Psalm 23 and wanted to inform you of my three girlfriends – Shirley, Goodness, and Mercy and their promise to follow me all the days of my life.

I also wanted you to know I mailed you a check to reimburse you for the airfare.

Thanks much!

Randy

Subject: Re: Good Morning
Date: 10/25

Randy,

I'm beginning to see why you have girls following you. I don't blame them. Thanks too for your call last night.

I forgot to tell you thanks for letting me know some of your plans for our 11/10 weekend. It looks great! Thanks for thinking ahead and for asking Sam if I could stay with them. I appreciate that. Remember too that you don't have to entertain me, I'm coming to hang out with you so we can get to know each other a little better. Whatever form that takes is fine with me.

Sam called me this morning to let me know that they were happy to have me stay with them when I visit you. What a breath of fresh air to have communication like that.

I had a powerful time of praying this morning with His conviction and presence. It makes me want to be with the Lord. I'm such a mess of emotions lately, but the Lord told me today, "Stay the course. I will keep you."

Susie is in Denver today with some more tests. How my heart is with her and asking for His mercy.

Thanks too for your "Hoosier" postcard and letter. I have heard one meaning of what a Hoosier is, but I'm researching further from a buried capsule under Indiana University's Assembly Hall.

Sandy

Subject: A long day
Date: 10/27

Hi, Randy.

Thanks for your concern, thoughts and prayers.

I took Susie home yesterday about 4:00 PM. Her cancer has returned and she is facing more chemotherapy and another major surgery. She was exhausted and had been crying most of the day. I realized she needed company, so we ordered pizza, got into our pajamas, and watched three no-brainer TV shows.

This morning we talked another two hours about all kinds of stuff. I also prayed with her.

Regarding your question about when did I first sense your interest in me? That is the $20,000 question. So for the curious . . . I knew during the fundraising seminar and from several things, tangible and intangible, but I did not know the extent of it. Also, Judie told me you had asked her some questions about me.

Thanks too for your stream of postcards. You are a nut.

Many blessings to you.

Who is your date to the Halloween party?

Sandy

Subject: A Nut and a Date
Date: 10/27

Good Afternoon, Lady Sandy,

Thanks for being there for Susie, I know she appreciates
everything you are doing.

Your emotional reservoir is amazing—Susie, work, team,
Marine, etc., etc.! May God continue to open the
floodgates.

About my "interest in you" question, I confess that I
asked Judie one question at lunch one day in the dining hall when we ended up sitting next to each other, "Is
Sandy married?" Judie replied, "No, but I think she would
like to be." It was music to my ears.

Now for the $64,000 question, would you care to elaborate
on your "tangibles and intangibles" in noticing my interest in you?

I asked Shirley, Goodness, and Mercy to the Halloween
Party but they all replied they would not follow me there.
So invited Solo and she agreed, though she required that I
wear a mask because of rumors she heard, even as far away
as Colorado, that I was a nut!

Nuts to you,

Randy

Subject: 50/50
Date: 10/27

To a man who is a nut,

Thanks for your call last night. I'm not sure if I made any sense because I was very tired, so disregard anything that fits that category. I was also wishing you were here.

My good friend Coleen is coming tonight from Denver to have dinner. She is also one of my former roommates. Looking forward to it!

And now we'll raise you and up the ante to $125,000 for those intangibles. My spiritual mentor Bobbi wants to know first when you were first interested in me. Then we'll split you 50/50.

Thinking of you,

Sandy

Subject: Worth Far Above Gold
Date: 10/30

To a Good Woman,

I enjoyed our time together last night on the phone. Praise God for quality friends like Bobbi and Coleen—precious moments of crying and laughing together. It is great medicine for the soul.

Regarding more about when I was interested in you, here are some tangibles, tangelos, intangibles, and tangerines for your consumption.

Right before I met you, the month of August was by far the most emotional month of my life. God was at work preparing me to meet you. I gave a 10-minute testimony at the Navigator Reunion with all these 80-year-old old godly men and women. When I thanked them for passing the baton to my generation, I lost it and cried.

The three trips I took to Colorado in August and September, along with the commissioning and prayers and testimonies from the seminar, were a multiple-year emotional release and emptying for me. I have never been overcome like that! I just read about Joseph in Genesis 45:1 this morning and remembered.

Plus the prayers that people prayed at Dawson Trotman's gravesite were heartfelt, and the individual and corporate committing to go all out for God rekindled some big emotions, and I lost it again.

First, let me begin by sharing this tangible: That the lovely and funny picture of you that you sent now has a gold frame around it and has a very prominent place on my desk.

My three trips to Navigator headquarters in August and September were for the Navigator staff conference, old-timers' Navigator Reunion, and the New Staff Orientation and fundraising seminar. First, during the staff conference, Nancy gave me a tour of all the office spaces at headquarters, including introducing me to your empty cubicle. I also recall connecting your name and acting ability in one of your stellar fundraising videos.

During the New Staff Orientation, I was introduced to you briefly while you were near the kitchenette. My next recollection was a brief conversation after the Income Accounting class, and I found out you were from Indiana. The above did not seem out of the ordinary, just meeting new people in a new place.

Flashback to four years ago, and God gave me a verse
from Job through one of my close mentors, Dan. I claimed
this verse for my past and future concerning a female
companion.

During the Orientation and fundraising seminar and my
times alone with God, the Holy Spirit would not allow that
memorized verse in Job to leave my brain. Most things
leave my brain very easily so I knew this to be unusual,
or said differently, of His doing.

Then came the fundraising seminar, and God opened my eyes
and heart and I became aware of YOU. Initially I denied
it and shied away from you thinking, "Lord, what are you
doing?"

I prayed, observed, cried, laughed, and prayed some more.
Out of the blue, at lunch, with a crowded table, I asked
Judie if you were married. After her response, I quickly
changed the subject. I observed your spirit, enthusiasm,
warmth, passion, poise, and fun like a hawk. My heart
began racing, "Lord, what are you doing?"

Again, out of the blue, at our team table during the seminar, I asked Gene and Marilyn about you. We got inter-
rupted before they could answer, and the program continued
with no response.

Then came the laser tag, car shenanigans, and the castle
bell tower foretaste of heaven. Deep admiration of you
welled up inside. I left a short post-it note on your
desk.

While flying home, in the window seat, I wrestled with God
about the Job verse and said, "But Lord, I don't even know
her." Finally, the Lord and His Spirit settled my heart
through Psalm 90:12, and told me to number my days, seek
Him and His wisdom by journaling for 30 days, concerning

you. I have been journaling for 30 days and it's been
neat!

The thirtieth day was last Saturday. Your and Bobbi's
question and turning the tables on me couldn't have been
more well-timed. I am free to share with you that God is
at work from my perspective, and I am thrilled! I think
you knew that already!

Have you seen or heard of the Romance Hand illustration?
The first two stages are Awareness and Admiration.

In conclusion, here is a short answer to my initial interest in you, for you and Bobbi. God used the fundraising
seminar to take me through the awareness and admiration
stages with flying colors.

So, are you ready to split 50/50 and answer your part?

Passionate about the Lord, ice cream, discipling, basketball, and YOU!

Randy

Subject: Shy hawk
Date: 10/30

Hi, Randy.

Thank you so much for your e-mail this morning sharing your heart,
feelings, and part of your story. I am honored, flattered, deeply
touched, and have goose bumps. Be assured that my attraction to you
is equally strong, even though I have some "issues along the way" to
think through and talk about with you.

You sure know how to make it hard for a girl to concentrate on her work.

Yes, I'm ready to split you 50/50. I'll e-mail you tonight with part of my story. Stay tuned. And stay encouraged by the One who loves us so.

Sandy

Chapter 6

The Next (Big) Step

With the many voices in our culture crying out for equality in everything, the benefits of masculinity and femininity in a relationship have been undercut and overlooked. The blurring of male/female roles can easily spawn confusion in relationships. While Scripture is clear that men and women are equal in eternal worth (Galatians 3:28), our Creator also fashioned complementary roles and strengths for each in unique and beautiful interdependence.

As women, in our good and innate quest for love, we can unwittingly undermine the wooing and initiative we long for from a man. That happens when we "cannot" wait another day for him to initiate, so we call and ask him to dinner. Or we text message him four times in one day to make sure he doesn't forget about us. Or we buy tickets to the concert Friday night before he has a chance to plan something for us. These may seem innocent enough, but they actually sabotage the very thing we desire—to be pursued and to see him take initiative.

Randy should write a book on how to pursue a woman. He was marvelous! From day one, he did not hide his interest in me. He asked questions that showed genuine interest in my life, work, and friendships. Always a gentleman, he opened doors for me, took initiative to write and call me, planned activities for us, and helped in practical ways—like with my car—without any strings attached. After Randy sought the Lord to confirm His leading, at the right time, he openly expressed his interest in me and his desire to move ahead with our relationship. He progressively shared from his life and heart in ways that invited me in. Never pushy, he allowed me space and time. His words and actions always demonstrated integrity, honesty, and purity. I sensed and observed that he enjoyed me for me.

Randy's pursuit of me was enhanced by a stream of funny and creative postcards. For a couple of months, I received a postcard almost daily. Many were hilarious, some were romantic, and many were creative as Randy simply spoke from his heart. I looked forward to them. Here are a couple of the postcards he sent me.

Looking for a creative way to send Randy a big thank you for the dozens of postcards he'd sent me, I hatched a plan. I determined to flood Randy's mailbox with a stack of postcards *in one day*. Recruiting friends to help, my goal was to send 50 postcards all at once. After setting it all up, I invited friends to write their own funny or creative sentences to Randy. He enjoyed the surprise of the pile of postcards that arrived that day.

While Randy wooed me long distance, several other things were pulling at my heart, time, and attention. One was caring for my friend Susie during her multiple cancer surgeries and rounds of chemotherapy. On top of that, her husband was unfaithful and unrepentant, and they were divorcing. Another good friend who lives in the Caribbean became engaged, and I was preparing to fly there to be the maid of honor in her wedding. I was also quietly job hunting but finally suspended this because of all the other things happening in my life. I decided to stay at my job for a while longer and see what would happen with Randy. Deep down, I already knew. In the midst of this intense roller coaster that was my life, how delicious it was to be pursued so clearly, so amazingly, so strongly.

Departure day to visit Randy grew closer, and my head was spinning at the speed of it all. My emotions charged ahead while my rational side attempted to maintain sense and sensibility. Excitement and nervousness competed as I also prepared to meet Randy's grown daughters for the first time. How would that go? What was each one like? Many times it all felt surreal, and I wondered if this was really happening.

Subject: 50/50
Date: 10/31

Randy,

It's Halloween, but no tricks tonight, only treats. Here is what I promised to answer for you—my side of the question, <u>when did I notice</u>

<u>your interest in me</u>?

When you signed up for the fundraising seminar, Judie found out you were single. She purposefully introduced you to me at the kitchenette just outside of my desk during the New Staff Orientation. I assumed you were married, so I didn't think anything of it. I remember saying hello and probably saying something about the upcoming seminar.

I also remember the Income Accounting session. I was out of touch a little with what staff were being taught at that session, so I chose to sit in on it to learn and evaluate it. It was also a chance to meet many of the staff prior to the seminar. I remember talking a little to you, but not the specifics.

Then the seminar started. I did not want to be there because I was frustrated with some things. I had actually thought earlier of asking to sit this one out, but I knew that would not be professional, and I did not want to let our team down. I just trusted God for the grace to focus.

Judie told me before the seminar started that you were single and that's why she had introduced you. I thought, okay here we go again, yeah, yeah. I have met other single men at seminars and had interest in a few, but nothing resulted afterward. Yet it also struck an old chord that it feels nice to be thought of, and maybe this time will be different.

I had an argument with God and ended up with, "Okay God, I'll give what I can to the seminar. I guess Judie was looking out for me, so I should be a little open. I won't avoid Randy. I'll be open if You want me to." I confess I also went into the meeting room early and set your notebook in a position where I knew I could see you in the meeting room. Figured it would help in observing. I was watching you some too.

Another factor in my argument with God was something from my summer in Russia. You know of the soap opera with one person. But there was also Don. In Russia, he flirted with me many times. I was fighting it inside because of what had just happened to me. But then I wondered if God was giving me something better, so I reciprocated interest.

But once we returned from Russia, I heard nothing from Don. Eventually I worked through that disappointment too and let it go. In September I re-read Proverbs 4:23. I had tried to protect my heart with Don and the man previous to him, but both of them had deceived me. I was determined to keep my heart and do things differently.

That was my state of mind coming into the seminar, and thus the 40-percent capacity in more ways than one. So I wasn't "looking."

But I noticed several things about you.
I saw you looking at me a few times.
Judie had told me you had asked about me. Something about this is always nice to hear.
I sat beside you at lunch once and you were nice.
When I gave you a copy of our sample funding letter, I could tell you did not want me to feel bad since Gene had already given you a copy. I saw a kind heart.
You came to my workshop and participated.
When we played the dice game Farkle, you seemed to enjoy it and seemed to be a little more relaxed.
When we were on the castle roof with those friends, I noticed you had stood back by yourself for a little while. I was going to invite you to join in and stand with us, but I didn't think I knew you well enough to say that.
I also saw that you made your way down to help the women onto the catwalk as we started to climb down from the bell tower. You were a gentleman, observant, and taking initiative.
One day you told me that you realized I had walked to my car at night by myself and that you should have offered to walk me there. That night I had wondered if you would offer to do just that. No problem that you didn't, but when you told me you had thought of it, I liked that.
At the ice cream time, you pulled out my chair to help seat me.

And for some reason you were paying attention to me.

I wondered if you were going to say goodbye to me after the seminar. When I saw your note saying "Thanks for everything," I liked that and sensed it was more than just a staff saying thanks for the seminar. Somehow I knew I would hear from you again and wasn't worried because I knew you would take the initiative.

Then I was very impressed with your e-mails. From your very first one, I loved it and saw you had a good sense of humor and wit. It was like a magnet. And all those first several e-mails were happening while I was rethinking a job change!

Your e-mails engaged me, and I began to see your heart and appreciated the openness of your interest. And with a little foundation of seeing you as a gentleman, a giving person, thoughtful and willing to take some initiative, I was more willing.

But it has been a tug of war. I am still fighting some things and know it will take me some time. I see much in you that draws me and that I admire. Yet we haven't been around each other that much! Looking back, I think my being about half capacity and feeling vulnerable actually made me more approachable. I was trying to be myself and get through the seminar.

And now, I'm coming to see you in 10 days! Thanks for the invite and your generosity. Haven't done this before either. But in spite of my crazy tug of war, I smile when I think of it, and of you.

Thanks for being you. You are pretty amazing.

Sandy

Subject: Pretty and Amazing

Date: 10/31

Sandy,

You sure know how to make a guy's Halloween!

I especially enjoyed your "costume": honest, transparent, genuine, and vulnerable. Scares some people but endears my heart. Thank you very much for sharing your heart, emotions, struggles, and issues of life.

My admiration and respect for you only deepens as I learn more of what you were going through before, during, and after the fundraising seminar.

Thanks for being obedient to God—He always blesses those who trust Him. Sounds like I owe Judie too. Please thank her for me for being sensitive to the Holy Spirit and to you.

Your e-mails and phone calls are the highlight of my days. I can't imagine what your visit will do to me!

The preparations of the heart, including all tugs of war, are from God. Proverbs 16:1

Good night dear one,

Randy

Subject: Notebook Arranger
Date: 11/2

Good Morning, Sandy!

As usual, neat talking to you last night. Can't wait to

see you in person!

Yes, I looked at you quite often during the fundraising seminar.

Thanks for your flight information. I will be there to pick you up either with the Presidential limo or with the chariot if I get time to grease the wheels. Do you have a preference?

I admire you for waiting and trusting God through your current work situation. Thanks also for your question last night about lessons I have learned. I enjoy being put on the spot. Feel free to ask away.

I am motivated about going to the one-day conference on Saturday and anxious to see some old military buddies.

I was also curious about your comment a while ago on the stage in your life where you did not like men. Or was it that you did not trust men?

I have to go now. Here's looking at you!

Psalm 63 – "I have seen you in the sanctuary and beheld your power and your glory. Because your love is better than life, my lips will glorify you."

Thanks for everything,

Randy

Subject: Grateful
Date: 11/3

Good morning, Randy.

My heart has been heavy this morning. God burdened me for Susie again. I had to let go and relinquish her to the Lord Jesus.

Tonight I am taking a friend out for her birthday.

Regarding your question about my stage in life where I did not like men—it was through some of my twenties that I didn't trust men and thus didn't like them. There were exceptions of course, but that was my frame of mind.

It's a long story, but looking back to when I was a teenager, I did not know how to do the dating thing. I did not get asked out much and had a poor self-image. I had a date with a hometown boy that went sour and left me with a very bad taste. It took a while to work through. Another man from high school was continually aggressive in trying to get alone with me. He wanted sex. I didn't. It pushed me into beginning to perceive all men were that way. I also saw that most men went for the cute ditzy girls, and I was not one of them.

In college a man tried to abduct me from a courtyard between some of the classroom buildings. He forced my arm behind my back, held something in his other hand that I assumed was a weapon, and started to push me forward. It happened in seconds. I screamed, then he let go, and I ran. Thankfully I got away from him. I had another man try to kiss me right in the dorm lobby area of a wild dorm where I had to live for awhile. He was a total stranger and totally drunk. That was disgusting.

So much of my initial encounters with men were negative. I definitely did not trust them nor care to be around them. But after I became a believer, God put me around some wonderful, caring, and honest men, and He began to change me. Eventually I forgave the high school episode, and that opened the door for me to move ahead. God was also beginning the long process of grounding my self-image in Him.

So that is a big part of how all those troubles began. I've grown much since then thanks to the Lord and several good friends who loved me and hung in there with me. Truth does set us free if we take it in and deal with the roots of our issues. What an incredible Savior we have. How I long to be with Him.

May the Lord also keep touching your soul too, like He did for you throughout those times in August. You mentioned feeling a release of some things. Have you thought more about those and what God is doing in you? No need to respond. It is just a question.

I don't mind your questions either. It is the path of becoming better friends. Thanks for caring.

Grateful, and your friend,

Sandy

Subject: Girls and Guys continued
Date: 11/3

Good evening, Sandy,

I trust you had a wonderful time with your friend as well. I hope all your friends don't mind if I steal you away for four days next week. If they do mind, tough!

Sorry I missed you on the phone tonight. I miss talking to you in person! Thanks also for being you—candid.

I'm continuing to pray with you and Susie—grace and wisdom.

Regarding my experience with girls and stuff, I not only didn't know how to do the dating thing, I didn't want to. Sports was my consuming passion. I did not ask girls out. I was shy and admired girls from a distance. I couldn't figure them out because I never really talked to them. Had a misconception that all girls were nice, innocent, feminine, kind, sensitive, non-manipulative, and non-deceitful. Hello!

I went to the Junior prom with a girl only because I didn't want my friends to think I couldn't get a date. I think I asked her out Monday before the Friday prom. It was not that much fun, and I put dating back on the shelf.

My self-image was wrapped up in what others thought of me, mainly on the athletic field. I played the big three (football, basketball, baseball) year-round so I couldn't get away from this wrong image of myself. If I played well, I thought I would be liked. If I didn't, I wouldn't. My significance as a person was manipulated by my perception of people's impression of me. Most of this time, this was a lose-lose situation.

I loved the game but didn't play much. Hence, I had a poor self-image and was shy. No confidence either. This only caused me to double my athletic efforts in hopes of attracting the interest of girls. The cute girls liked the jocks, or so it seemed.

Enter Jesus Christ. He knew me, accepted me unconditionally, and even loved me with or without skills. Oh, my God, I love you so! Thank you, Lord. That love and confidence changed me forever. Freed up my spirit to learn to be me and like me.

I gained some confidence. I had one girl interested in high school, but it was not due to much initiative on my part. She was a transfer student and was assigned to the back of the alphabet with the Ws. God used me to "nag" her into His kingdom. We graduated, went to separate colleges, and eventually broke up as she became more dependent on me than on the Lord.

I did not date much in college. I joined the Marine Corps

out of college. Met my former wife in church in North
Carolina. I believe she still struggles with an unbiblical
self-image today, and I believe this is one of the root
causes of why she made the choices she did and why she has
experienced serious consequences.

Adultery, emotional estrangement, abandonment of husband
and children, and her subsequent divorce did not shatter
my confidence in God or His sovereignty. Of course I was
crushed and devastated at the betrayal and deceitfulness.
I always believed she would repent and eventually return.
But she did neither.

It has been said that men derive their worth from work
while women tend to derive their worth from relationships.
Both leave out the core of Christ.

I am extremely loyal. The nature of the second-born
is loyalty. My training is faithfulness. God's nature
is faithfulness, and I am required to be like Him in
faithfulness.

It's late, so sorry if I'm wandering. I have forgiven my
ex-wife and harbor no bitterness. God has released me from
that commitment after ten years of waiting on Him, not
her. There is much biblical evidence for remarriage if God
should so lead.

Though I am still trying to sort out the onslaught of my
August emotions, I believe that was one of the areas.
Another area is God's timing for His call on my life
to serve in full-time missions. While in the Corps, I
resigned my commission three times to get out and serve
with Navigators, but each time God closed the door. It was
what I call the triple death of a vision. I learned to
keep waiting on Him.

Another emotional release point for me was a feeling of
unconditional love from the Master, enveloped in His personal arms.

Another—my heart was being prepared by God Himself to love another.
Another—the release from the divorce stigma and the lie that God can't or won't use me because of it.
Another—the importance of commitment to a team, wisdom of a team, accountability of a team, and power of a team.

I had better go, it's after 11:00 and I need to get up early. There is more to say, but I just ran out of time. So why don't you come out for a visit?

Oh, how I do love God!

Randy

Subject: Prom date
Date: 11/5

Hi, Randy.

I was never asked to the prom at all. So I was thinking, if you would like to go to the senior prom, I believe I'm free this weekend. It could be a lot of fun.

I would love to come for a visit. In fact, this guy I know is paying my way. What a chum. I am nervous, excited, and everything in between.

Thanks for your e-mail and more of your story. Appreciate you sharing it. I woke up this morning thinking of you. We have similarities during those crazy teen years. Thank God that in time, He chose to show us that there is no other anchor besides Him. I wish I never struggled anymore with image or fear issues, but the key is going back to the anchor.

I had a great time with God today. Finished reading 2 Samuel and into I Kings. It's amazing that for hundreds of years, God would choose to not show Himself very often in a tangible way, then show His presence in a traveling tabernacle, and then display His presence in a magnificent temple. There is such a pull for us to want to see Him. And now He chooses to dwell in us! Hard to fathom.

I have to go now to one more birthday party for a few hours.

May God fill your heart and give you some rest as you have given much to people this weekend.

His and yours,

Sandy

Subject: Prom Acceptance
Date: 11/5

Sandy,

Yes, I accept and will take you to the prom. I'll pick you up, say 10:30 Friday! I'm convinced we'll have fun. I can identify with all your emotions, and then some. In my daughter's words, "Just kick back!"

I remember thinking about asking you to come out for a visit and then hesitating, thinking that it's too early and I should not rush things. But then three days later, I asked you! Within 24 hours, you said yes. Oh, thank God for feelings and emotions.

Thanks for sharing your neat insights and time with God with me. I am interested in hearing about God's promises to you and what you are trusting God for. I'd enjoy sharing mine with you too.

I have going to church on Saturday with you on the schedule for a couple of reasons. One of them is so I can listen to you sing, a thrill for me.

Bless you!

A chum who likes you

Subject: Visiting is a good idea
Date: 11/6

Randy,

When you first asked me to come out to visit, I thought it was cute,
and that you had courage to ask. You said you wanted to spend some
time with me—made me smile. You were just finding out about the
struggles of my team situation, and you offered a place to get away
if I needed to. Appreciated that even though I knew I had to stay and
work it through.

I was surprised that your invitation came so soon. I thought, "This guy
doesn't waste any time!" But Bobbi had already asked me, "So, Sandy,
when are you going to invite Randy out?" I thought, oh yeah, I guess I
should think about that.

As I was thinking through when to see you, my yo-yo brain said: "I
like this...WHAT AM I DOING?...but he has a good heart...but I don't
know him that well...this seems so fast." A friend at work asked me
how I was doing with you, so I told her the yo-yo scenarios and she
replied, "You need some time with him." That confirmed it for me, and
I e-mailed you that day or the next. Usually being a low risk taker and
someone who adjusts slowly to big change, I wondered later if it was
still a good idea. But now I know it is!

I have a thought about this weekend. It will help me relax if we take our expectations and lower them a notch. It seems there is so much to talk about that it's overwhelming. I'm sure it will be a wonderful combo of things. Very excited to see you!

I won't tell Sam that you might not be paying attention in church. I look forward to seeing where you have been going to church, and if you wear socks to church or not.

Have fun folding, signing, and stamping your letter, and put on some good music. Naps in between are approved.

Your friend and fan,

Sandy

Subject: Expectation Meter
Date: 11/7

Good morning, Sandy!

Thanks for your precious heart and thanks for sharing your feelings in yesterday's e-mail. I really appreciate your straightforwardness and candor.

Let's turn down the expectation meter as much as we can. That's a wise idea. Please be assured that we can and will do whatever you want out here. The schedule and itinerary is wide open and can be scrapped at a moment's notice.

You have had a stressful situation at work and your deep personal relationship with Susie and her condition have been trying. Then along comes this Marine. . . . So, our number-one objective is to have fun, relax, and get to know each other a little more. I've also booked tickets for us to see the play Dracula, which may not sound that appealing, but I've heard it is not scary, but a mild, well-done story.

One of my life verses is Psalm 62:5-8: "My soul, wait thou only upon God; for my expectation is from Him. He only is my rock and my salvation: He is my defense; I shall not be moved."

And my old standby is Psalm 73:25-26, well-used in my many times of need. "Whom have I in heaven but Thee? And there is none upon earth that I desire besides Thee. My flesh and my heart may fail; but God is the strength of my heart and my portion forever."

I have volunteered you as a guest singer in our church. No pressure and no expectations. It's your choice of song.

I have a neat story I'm going to send you later. You'll need your Kleenex.

Voting for you,

Randy

Subject: A Good Seed
Date: 11/7

Sandy,

Here is a story I thought you would like.

John Blanchard stood up from the bench, straightened his Army uniform and studied the crowd of people making their way through Grand Central Station. He looked for the girl whose heart he knew, but whose face he didn't, the girl with the rose. His interest had begun thirteen months before in a Florida library. Taking a book off the shelf he found himself intrigued, not with the words of the book, but with notes penciled in the margin. The soft handwriting reflected a thoughtful soul and an insightful mind. In the front of the book, he discovered the previous owner's name, Miss Hollis Maynell. With time and effort he located her address. She lived in New York City. He wrote a letter introducing himself and inviting her to correspond. The next day he was shipped overseas in World War II.

During the next year and one month the two grew to know each other through the mail. Each letter was a seed falling on a fertile heart. A romance was budding. Blanchard requested a photograph, but she refused. She felt that if he really cared, it wouldn't matter what she looked like. When the day came for him to return from Europe, they scheduled their first meeting—7:00 PM at the Grand Central Station in New York. She wrote, "You'll recognize me by the red rose I'll be wearing on my lapel." So at 7:00 he was in the station looking for a girl whose heart he loved, but whose face he'd never seen.

I'll let Mr. Blanchard tell you what happened.

A young woman was coming toward me, her figure long and slim. Her blonde hair lay back in curls from her delicate ears: her eyes were as blue as cornflowers. Her lips and chin had a gentle firmness, and in her pale green suit she was like springtime come alive. I started toward her, entirely forgetting to notice that she was not wearing a rose.

As I moved, a small provocative smile curved her lips. "Going my way, soldier?" she murmured. Almost uncontrollably I made one step closer to her, and then I saw Hollis Maynell. She was standing almost directly behind the girl. A woman well past 40, she had graying hair tucked under a worn hat. She was more than plump, her thick-ankled feet thrust into low-heeled shoes. The girl in the green suit was walking quickly away. I felt as though I was split in two, so keen was my desire to follow her, and yet so deep was my longing for the woman whose spirit had truly companioned me and upheld my own.

And there she stood. Her pale, plump face was gentle and sensible, her gray eyes had a warm and kindly twinkle. I did not hesitate. My fingers gripped the small worn blue leather copy of the book that was to identify me to her. This may not be love, but it would be something precious, something perhaps even better than love, a friendship for which I had been and must ever be grateful. I squared my shoulders and saluted and held out the book to the woman even though while I spoke I felt choked by disappointment. "I'm Lieutenant John Blanchard, and you must be Miss Maynell. I am so glad you could come and meet me; may I take you to dinner?"

The woman's face broadened into a tolerant smile. "I don't know what this is about, son," she answered, "but the young lady in the green suit who just went by, she begged me to wear this rose on my coat. And she said if you were to ask me out to dinner, I should go and tell you that she is waiting for you in that big restaurant across the street. She said it was some kind of a test."

It is not difficult to understand and admire Miss Maynell's wisdom. The true nature of a heart is seen in its response to the unattractive. "Tell me whom you love," Houssaye wrote, "And I will tell you who you are."

For the One who is altogether Lovely,

Randy

Subject: Re: A Good Seed
Date: 11/7

Randy,

Let us clone Hollis Maynell and John Blanchard many times over. Of course appearance and looks we notice, but without question the greatest attraction any day is a good heart. A wonderful story indeed!

Well, I haven't been asked to go see Dracula in a long time. You romantic you. But if you're going, I'm going. At first, I thought you were kidding about Dracula, but it sounds like the real McCoy, which is fine.

Also, regarding singing at your church – I'll need about an hour to prepare for singing Saturday night. Possibilities include:
She Wears a Size 11 Shoe, But I Still Like Her
He Can't Sing or Dance, But He Can Spell Avocado

And regarding your wanting to set a time to call me:
The lady of Bourke Street requesteth
Said Prom Date to call this nighteth of 7 November
Say around 9:30 starlight mountain timeth.
She shouldest be home from the Cactus Rose fine dinery
Saying farewelleth to the quaint company of Lady Susie and her doctor
Only to accompany Lady Susie home to a peroxide extravaganza.

If any questions about the peroxide, Lady Susie's unusual friend with a size 11 shoe, Susie's number is 444/222-3333 or 1-800-YESSIREE.

Talk with you soon!

Sandy

(Susie and I really are going out to dinner tonight with one of Susie's doctors. Solely as friends, but she did not want to go by herself.)

Subject: Bread and Butter
Date: 11/8

Good Morning, Soon To Be Passenger,

"Dad, you're not that special; why is Sandy freaking out
about coming to see you?" Quote from my daughter, Miss
Merrilee. Nothing like a little affirmation, huh?

Thanks for your special e-mail after a long day for you.
You're so thoughtful!

My Thursday sounds like your Wednesday:
Meet with two pastors
Clean carriage to pick up Sandy
Two late-night basketball games
Call American Airlines to change your Monday departure to
Saturday
Measure my shoe size against a size 11
Practice my Kingeth James language
Learn to sing and dance or learn to spell avocado
Peroxide my hair and make it a team function
Coordinate your singing prep during Dracula intermission
Order some relaxers

The San Diego Zoo is world famous and a must-see. Sea
World is a lot of fun as well. When are you coming for a
re-visit?

I want to hear about your trip to Kenya sometime too. Also
thanks for sharing some of your verses. I will call you
Thursday to touch base. Time to sleep.

Have a tremendous day,

Randy

Subject: Of Courage
Date: 11/8

Randy,

What a day today. Solid meetings.

Glad you liked Toy Story 2. My favorite part is the out-takes at the end. Thanks too for all the postcards! What a wit you have. They are on my desk, and I look at them often.

Appreciate your comments on the "courage" of me coming out to San Diego to see you. Though I'm still a bit of a yo-yo, I'm more glad and excited!

Another life verse for me: Isaiah 60:21,22—"Then all your people will be righteous; they will possess the land forever, the branch of My planting, the work of My hands, that I may be glorified. The smallest one will become a clan, and the least one a mighty nation. I, the Lord, will hasten it in its time."

Also, for the Miss Merrilee of your house, please tell her . . .
Just wait until it happens to you.
Then I shall smile and say,
Hey, just kick back.
Why are you so nervous?
After all, he can spell Jesus and avocado,
He can e-mail and use the telephone
He doesn't eat pizza every night at home
And he is not afraid to watch ice skating.
He appears to have passed his college exams,
Including the infamous English 404 turn 'em out term papers.

He stopped smoking cigars two weeks ago
And he is not afraid to wear a pink shirt, that is, once every ten years.
So how bad can he be?

Of courage and of the Holy One,
Ready or not, here I come.

From a Colorado connection who knows how to relax AND have fun too.

Chapter 7

Face to Face

Day One

Boarding the plane for my three-and-a-half-day trip to see Randy, I was an excited mess. No question we were both strongly attracted to one another's hearts, yet what about the day-to-day realities of being together? Long-distance dating cuts out the everyday-life stuff, and a romantic ideal can easily be fantasized as real relationship—or substituted for it. True rapport has to be worked out in the realities of being together, day in and day out. You want to naturally observe things, such as: How does he communicate in person? How does he present himself? What is he like in his own environment? With his friends? Am I physically attracted to him? Do I think I could live with this man? Does he drive his car like a maniac? How does he interact with others? Do I enjoy his company? How does he handle conflict? Any weird habits? Is there authenticity? What kind of father would he be to my children? Do I truly respect him? Because we had not been around one another much, Randy and I definitely needed to be able to answer these questions about each other.

In my window seat on the plane, I read in Psalms to help me calm down. Having high motion sensitivity, I take Dramamine when traveling, but it makes me sleepy. I certainly didn't want to feel groggy when I got off the plane to meet my handsome prince, so I simply had to ask the Lord to dissipate any queasiness. When the plane began the descent, my mind kicked into high gear. *"Should I hug him? What should I say? How do I look?"*

Walking off the plane, weak-kneed and heart pounding, suddenly I forgot all of the questions I wanted to ask Randy. I saw him standing there with a warm smile and a rose. He greeted me, arms out for a gentle hug, then handed me the rose. (What a gentleman!) My stomach was still in knots, but small talk broke the ice. One of my first secret impressions was, *"I thought you were taller!"*

After getting situated in Randy's well-worn Honda, he asked, "Sandy, would you get my wallet out of the glove box, please?" A little surprised, I lifted the latch to pop open the glove box, and I jumped. Inside was a fake left arm! This eased my crazy jitters.

Randy drove to nearby, beautiful Seaport Village in downtown San Diego. We ordered lunch and sat at an outdoor café table. Randy offered his hand when he prayed to thank God for the meal. The few seconds of my hand in his felt wonderful! After more chitchat, we left to walk and talk for a while, offering the detailed versions of how we came to know Jesus Christ as our Savior and Lord.

After a while, Randy had planned a nearby harbor cruise. The tour guide started off fine but quickly grew annoying. Still, I felt warm all over simply standing next to Randy. After docking and de-boarding, the cruise company offered to take our picture, and it became our first photograph together. We walked and talked more, telling one another about our families and jobs among other things. How incredible it was to finally be able to talk in person! No doubt I got in my 60,000 words for the day! So did introvert Randy.

For dinner, we joined Randy's colleagues, who had opened their house to me, at the Spaghetti Factory. I had met Sam before, and thankfully he and his wife were enjoyable and easy to be around.

After dinner, tiredness cascaded over me from little sleep the night before and an early morning, but off we headed to a play. It was what every woman dreams of seeing—Dracula! Honestly, I didn't care what the play was, but it was at a small, quaint Christian theater and was tastefully done. They presented Dracula as more of a historical figure with no overt creepiness. At the theater, Randy wanted to put his arm around me, but decided to hold off on this first day of being together. I was fighting heavy sleepiness during the first act, realizing how embarrassing it would be to fall asleep on our first date! Thankfully a second wind bolstered me for the second half. How new and odd to suddenly be in a couples' environment, to like Randy, and to embrace the wave of sensory input that came from actually being around him. Today was our first day together as a couple. What a stark contrast from the singles scene!

In groups of singles, I often either felt like I was being "checked out" or that I was the odd man out, the "third wheel." (Once when I was in my late twenties or early thirties, friends who had invited couples over for dinner put me, the only single, at another table with their teenage children!)

With Randy, I felt noticed, liked, together. Later I observed that some couples related to me differently now that I was part of a couple. It's hard to describe, but they somehow seemed more interested and welcoming of me.

When Randy drove me to Sam and Shirley's house later that night, he gave me a gift after we pulled into the driveway. It was a framed picture of the small group of us who had hiked up to the castle rooftop and sung praise songs together. I loved it! Grateful and impressed, I wanted to hug Randy or hold his hand, but I also knew we should gradually ease into that. I waited and wondered when that time would come. The anticipation was exciting! My overtiredness won out over my feelings of bliss, and I was actually able to sleep that night.

Day Two

Randy picked me up at 9:00 the next morning. I was still not fully awake but ready for a day's adventure. We strolled the lovely Oceanside Pier and talked about things like my challenging work situation and our friends. I loved seeing and hearing the incredible ocean waves and watching the surfers. We paused and took a few pictures. When we left the pier, a stranger handed us a Christian tract, "The Greatest Love Story." It captured how we felt too.

Walking back to the car, we saw a police officer writing us a parking ticket! Silly, distracted us—we'd forgotten to put money in the meter. The officer relented. After shaking the sand from our shoes and getting into the car, Randy gave me a gift, a hilarious squeeze toy dubbed a "Sack of Potatoes." At that time, I decided to give Randy a belated birthday present that I had brought from Colorado, a mounted, singing fish called Big Mouth Billy Bass. Neither of us competent adults could open the sealed plastic carton to put the batteries in.

We drove to meet Randy's youngest daughter, Merrilee, at Circuit City where she worked. She was her wonderful, extroverted self, and we chitchatted for several minutes. I simply tried to be myself and was so very glad to finally meet her. I could tell right away she was a go-getter, competent, and very friendly. When we left she said, "Pops, it's so good to see you smiling again."

Spontaneously, we decided to leave Merrilee a funny note on her pickup truck for a good laugh. We scribbled something like, "If you wait until you are 30 to get married, you'll get a brand new truck with lots of extras," and tucked it under the windshield wiper.

Grabbing sandwiches for lunch, we drove to Randy's apartment. There I was thrilled to meet Mirachelle, Randy's middle daughter who was in college. Both Mirachelle and Merrilee lived at home with Randy. Mirachelle sweetly handed me a note of welcome and three balloons. How thoughtful! I discovered she likes to cook, so I asked her about that. After lunch, she showed me around the apartment. Both Mirachelle and Merrilee forewarned me that the apartment lacked a feminine touch. They were right! Mirachelle gave me a tour of her dad's many bookshelves, and I stifled my surprised laughter when we ended in Randy's room and found even more stuffed bookcases and file cabinets. The walls of the hallway were crowded with laminated pictures of the girls from their school activities and with friends. This showed me how Randy valued and loved his family. Most hilarious was an old console television in the tiny living room that produced a crooked picture and faulty audio. Randy was no slave to technology.

Randy then showed me a couple of picture albums. One was from the trip he took to Indiana to visit basketball sites. I observed his genuine love of the game as he glowingly talked about the trip. I noticed his attention to trip details.

I was beginning to relax. Meeting two of Randy's daughters made them more real to me, and I wanted to get to know them better. On this visit, I did not get to meet his oldest daughter, Alicia, who was already living on her own. More clearly, I started to see Randy not merely as "my man," but as a family man, a dad who continued to care for and support his girls through their adult lives.

Later we headed off to early afternoon church, where I met some of Randy's friends. Afterward, Randy drove me around Fallbrook, the town where he and his daughters had lived the past several years. It was like a slice of small-town life outside of suburban Southern California. Next we drove through the neighboring Marine Corps base, Camp Pendleton. Randy was retired from the Corps but had spent several years working at Pendleton, a huge base boasting miles of open, dry, hilly acres.

Dinner was at Claim Jumper, where the food comes in portions that threaten to overflow the plate. Here I asked Randy to tell me the story of his former marriage and divorce. He took his time, and I asked a lot of questions. With tears, he recalled those very painful years. I sniffled too, identifying with his pain. His former wife had an affair with a friend of Randy's, a man he was spiritually mentoring. Randy came home on emergency leave while deployed overseas, and just a couple days later, his wife left the house, left Randy and the children, and never returned. She eventually filed for divorce. Stunned, I felt heartbroken for Randy and each of the girls.

In those few hours, my respect for Randy skyrocketed as I heard how he dealt with such tragedy. When he told me he had since forgiven his former wife and his friend, harbored no bitterness, and had moved on, I could see that was true. I also asked Randy what he had learned from such a devastating ordeal. After three hours of talking, we were so wrung out and spacey that we left our delicious leftovers on the table.

Randy drove me back to Sam and Shirley's house. While sitting in the car, he reached into the backseat and brought out another wrapped gift. This time it was a more serious gift, beautiful candles. Deeply touched by the whole day, I quietly rested my head on his shoulder. He put his arm around my shoulder, and it felt wonderful and right. Gently, he leaned down and lightly kissed the top of my head. After a few quiet minutes lingering in one another's company, thankful for an awesome day together, he walked me to the door to say goodnight. We hugged and he gently kissed my cheek. A symphony broke out inside me! After a brief greeting to my hosts, I called my girlfriend in Colorado to tell her some of "the drama." Though tired, I jotted down a few of my thoughts, not wanting to forget all I was taking in and experiencing.

My head hit the pillow, spinning but utterly content. This Saturday had been grand, but I couldn't have guessed that the next day would be the most romantic day of my life.

Day Three

Randy picked me up Sunday morning, and we headed out to catch the ferry to beautiful Catalina Island for the day. After getting out of the car, we had a few minutes to wait for the ferry. We walked to a bench overlooking the ocean, and I naturally slipped my arm into Randy's arm. Sitting on the bench, looking out at the beautiful Pacific Ocean, I lightly stroked Randy's shoulder. He gently caressed my arm and knee. Couldn't we just stay in this moment forever?

When it was time to catch the ferry, we walked to the boarding dock. On the way, Randy held my hand, and it felt as natural as if we had known each other for years! The 90-minute ferry ride provided more time to talk. As the chilly breeze whipped by, I sat blissfully tucked under Randy's arm the whole way. I was so happy it was hard to think. Yet deep down I was anxious because it was our last full day together, which meant I had to bring up a topic that I feared. For me, it was a "make-or-break" issue, and it would be easy to chicken out. If the answer was no, I couldn't bear it; yet at the same time, I had to know.

But first I brought up some other issues. With only a couple days together, there was so much to communicate; it hardly seemed fair to feel such pressure in the midst of such bliss. My purpose in sharing these things was not so that Randy would solve anything, but I simply thought it would help him understand the rumblings inside me. First, I told him that I was not used to men staying around. This nasty fear lurked from years of getting my hopes up, only to have it not work out again, and watch the man move on. I also mentioned that I knew quite well how to be single, but I did not know how to be a couple yet! That sounds silly thinking about it today, but it was an issue for me then. After years of making my own decisions regarding finances, personal and professional goals, travel, and so forth, I worried a little about losing some freedom. I also told Randy that it was initially difficult to accept him paying for my plane ticket. Having lived independently for so long, it was hard to believe that this was real, that someone actually liked me and was incredibly nice to me, without feeling that I owed him something for it. Yet deep down I knew that this was good and right and I could simply embrace and enjoy it!

Randy asked me several things too. How did I feel about him being divorced? How did I feel about him being ten years older than me? I explained how God had worked in my heart already, and that neither was a deal-breaker.

Strolling around Catalina hand in hand, we took in the sights and snapped a few pictures. During lunch at a pizzeria, I thought, *"Sandy, ask Randy your question now or you will never do it."* I had wanted children all my life, and the lack of opportunity to marry and have children was a giant sorrow I bore. A couple of times in my late thirties, I had considered adopting a child. However, each of those times as excitement mounted and I asked for the Lord's direction, I sensed in my spirit that the Lord said, *"No, not now."* Disappointed and not fully understanding, I yielded to my Father and waited. Now a few years later, I was meeting the man of my prayers while my body clock ticked away loudly in the background. Since Randy had already raised three daughters, would he want any more children? If not, I could not bear it.

With my insides churning, I finally mustered the courage to tell Randy about my lifelong dream to have children, to have a family. Sitting at the picnic table after lunch, I said I didn't know what to do with that dream now since he had already been down that road. Whew, I finally said it!

The dread of hearing a "No thanks, I don't want any more children," halted everything inside me, making me feel limp. The next few seconds seemed like hours. I about fell off my chair when Randy grinned and responded, "Well, there's not a son to keep the Weyeneth name." Seconds later he followed with, "Oh, I did not mean to put any pressure on you." I was flabbergasted and overwhelmed. He was open to having more children! I could barely think or respond.

Our lunch ended with Randy telling me about a friend and former supervisor of mine whom he had contacted to find out more about me. While starting to describe what "Bruce" had said about me, Randy choked up, overcome with emotion, and could not continue. Later Randy would e-mail me what he had learned from Bruce.

After our rather intense lunch, we rented a golf cart and motored around the island at a whopping 10 mph. When I told Randy that I did not like to read maps, he said, "You drive, and I'll read the map." What a guy! He put his arm around me the whole time, and I loved it. Suddenly, it was not hard to let him pay for my meals, pay for my airfare, and take care of things for me, for us. For the first time, I felt like an "us," and it was fabulous, right, and a big part of what I was made for.

We parked the golf cart and ordered some ice cream. Unknowingly, I chose Randy's favorite flavor, which he knew to be another sign from God. We walked some more and ended up back at the pier by late afternoon, waiting for the return ferry back to Dana Point. As Randy stood behind me, I leaned against his chest, his arms tucked around my waist, and we stood gazing at the gorgeous harbor. Randy gently nudged his face against my head, then softly buried his face in my hair and barely whispered, "How could I not notice you?"

I simply melted. Wanting like crazy to turn around, I willed myself to stay put, knowing that if I turned to face Randy, we might kiss on the lips. Of course I wanted to, but we both understood that it was something special, and we wanted to wait until the right time. So I stayed nestled in his arms, longing to linger in this moment. Without a doubt, I knew that Randy loved me!

On the ferry ride back, we simply enjoyed the realization of God's good and faithful hand to give us the gift of one another.

We arrived at my hosts' home and visited with them for a bit. No doubt we two yo-yos made little sense then. How utterly hard it was to say goodbye to Randy that night. Gently hugging him goodbye, I told him I would miss him, for tomorrow I had to fly back to Colorado. How unfair that seemed now that we had found each other. After waiting all my life, I had finally found real relationship with this man, and now I had to leave him.

Day Four

My flight left Monday afternoon. We drove to a staff meeting that

Randy had with his team that morning. Although we hadn't planned to stay long, we ended up there for a bit and prayed together as a group. Then it was time for Randy to drive me to the airport.

That was a long ride. Choked with emotion, we tried talking, but it was hard. I don't remember much of what we said. Quite spacey after checking in and getting my boarding pass, I noticed United Airlines had made a mistake and failed to book me through to Colorado Springs. I returned to the counter to clear it up. Silly me. I had two boarding passes in my ticket holder, including the second leg of the trip to Colorado Springs, and had been too distracted to notice.

With only 10 or 15 minutes left together, I leaned against Randy, trying to write thank-you notes to Merrilee and Mirachelle. Randy gently stroked my arms with his face nestled against my hair. Somehow I managed to finish the notes, trying hard to hold it together. I cry very easily and knew that if I locked eyes with tear-streaked Randy, I would completely fall apart, and likely miss my flight.

When the dreaded boarding call came, it took everything I had to hug Randy and walk onto the plane. As the flight attendant took my ticket, I turned and waved one last goodbye, tears falling as I headed for my seat. They continued the whole flight home. Unable to talk or read, I was overcome by God. Love had bloomed. God was faithful in giving me what He had promised in a way only He could do.

Subject: Red Light/Green Light
Date: 11/14

Dearest Sandy,

Good morning, afternoon, and evening! Thanks for a wonderful weekend and all the sacrifices you made to venture out west.

My heart bubbles over! Thanks for your call last night—it was so satisfying to hear your voice after an emotional day for me. Sorry you had to come home to a cold home, but I did my best to warm your heart when you were here.

Did you every play red light/green light when you were young? You had to stop on red and could only go on green. Want to play?

I got up early this morning knowing I needed to hear from the Leader. I debated again as to whether to initiate communication with you. My heart was flashing bright green but my head said, "Go to God. So I did. Before I share my time with Him with you, I want to say, please also hear from God yourself. I know you will, and I respect and know that you will only do what He wants. It is easy to begin communication like this with you again, and once we start, it will be very difficult for me to stop. So take a deep breath, process His hand over this past weekend, seek His face, and know that whatever He shows you is good.

Maybe you want to take some days or weeks to seek the Lord. I'm on your side and support you totally. I want to be sensitive to the Spirit and to you. It's His relationship. We belong to Him, and He brings these crossroads in His time.

I reviewed Proverbs 4:23 and asked what does it mean to guard my heart? Because my heart influences everything else in life, I can only allow God's desires in there or I will be led astray. God promises that if I delight in Him, He will give me the desires of my heart because His desires have become my desires. What are His desires?

"My son, give me thine heart and let thine eyes observe my ways." He desires surrender and obedience daily.

"Whom have I in heaven but Thee?. . . God is the strength of my heart and my portion forever." No man or woman can totally meet the needs of the other, for only God can do that. God created us to need Him. If we look to a person to meet those needs, we will be frustrated. With that said, God does use a spouse to meet many needs, and that is His beautiful plan of marriage. It's His idea and was His plan before creation.

"In Thy presence is fullness of joy." I like to view it in the triangle illustration. God is at the apex, and husband and wife are in the other two corners. As each person continues to grow in their relationship with God, they inevitably grow closer to God until the three become one. That will ultimately take place at glorification; but two becoming one spiritually is the process of sanctification.

And what a beautiful and holy analogy He provides with the explanation of physical and sexual oneness. Interestingly, God uses the word "to know" to describe physical oneness in Genesis. Adam "knew" his wife Eve and she conceived. To know Him and to know you.

So I've given my heart and expectations to Him afresh—Psalm 62:5-6. With that background, I want to be bold and take the initiative and tell you that I've been very encouraged this morning in my time in the Word and prayer concerning you.

You are very beautiful to me in every sense of the word. I've asked God to play red light/green light with me. He keeps saying "Go." I know He knows the rules, and He could even throw in a yellow if He wants.

An example may be helpful. Flashback to your visit Sunday afternoon, while eating lunch at the Catalina pizzeria, I got choked up when sharing what Bruce answered concerning you. I re-read his e-mail that said, "I trust you my friend, Sandy is a wonderful woman and I am always amazed at how deep and talented she is."

Now I see from my own observation that it is not just flattery, but true! But what made me cry was something that

God overwhelmed my mind and heart with. Being in your presence was used by the Holy Spirit to make me want to be as holy as I possibly could. That shattered me and broke me and humbled me to the point of tears. Praise be to God and thanks for your life. I am still enjoying that brokenness and awe. It looks like a caseload of Kleenex will be necessary.

I realize that we didn't spend much time together in the Word and prayer, and I long for that in His time. But we did share how God has spoken to us in the past through those two means. To be honest, I think you have to be careful when praying together, and so I passed on that this last weekend.

With deep admiration,

Yo-Yo

Subject: An Admirer
Date: 11/14

Hello, Mr. Sweetheart.

Being very tired when I arrived home last night, I decided to sleep in until I woke up. I got into the office mid-morning and feel like I am in a dream world.

THANK YOU for so many things. For being you. For an absolutely wonderful weekend. Loved it all. Found it difficult to wake up this morning and not have you come and pick me up! Thought of you a great deal. For all the things we did . . . dinner together, boat rides, golf cart rides, Dracula, church, Catalina, lots of walking and talking. Thanks for coming to get me. For your honesty. For telling me your story. For letting me meet Merrilee and Mirachelle. I look forward to meeting Alicia too.

Thanks for showing me your pictures and telling me some of your stories. I enjoyed the candles, picture, funny "sack of potatoes," and yo-yo . . . how thoughtful you are!

I am truly amazed and utterly grateful that God has brought us together because I have waited and prayed for so long, I did not think it possible. But you have definitely made me think it possible. You have wooed my heart so beautifully. And I deeply admire YOU!

Do not worry, I will seek God. I am passionate for Him and like you, I must hear from Him. I have every confidence that He will speak in His time.

Thanks for sharing some of what God has brought your way with the Word. I look forward to more of the same for us both.

Regarding playing red light/green light . . . yes, count me in.

Here's something funny. I put the "sack of potatoes" toy in my briefcase. When I opened the garage door, threw in my briefcase and started the car, I jumped in fear after hearing someone's voice! Then I laughed, realizing it was the sack of potatoes talking!

Flashback to leaving yesterday. I got quiet at the airport because it is also hard for me to say goodbye. And I knew that if I looked at you, I would cry hard. I was thinking how wonderful you are. And how wonderful you have been to me. How I wanted to stay. I didn't know what to say. I wanted to stay in your arms.

Your tears moved me deeply. My tears came streaming down when I got on the plane. Tears of joy. Tears of sadness to have to leave.

I am with you. I am for you. And I am thrilled.

Admiring you,

Sandy

Subject: O Worship the King
Date: 11/15

Dear Lovely Lady,

I miss getting up and driving to pick you up! Got the CD
"O Worship the King" so I can listen to worship songs and
talk to you.

I'm wearing my Indiana Hall of Fame shirt today with the
word Indiana across my heart. I miss you bunches—when are
you coming again?

Word for the Day—"And hope does not disappoint, because
the love of God has been poured out within our hearts
through the Holy Spirit who was given to us." What is the
relation of the work of the Holy Spirit in our lives and
the amount of the love of God in our lives? Holiness and
Love—I'll take as much as I can get.

The girls think you are really cool. Finally, they believe
something Dad says! I responded to their question, "Did
you kiss her?" with "No, not on the lips." I sure wanted
to, but that is reserved for a special time later. Both
say thanks for the candy you gave them.

Thanks for your admiration—that means a lot to me! I too
am very affectionate. What a thrill to hold you in my
arms!

I greatly admire your prayer and waiting on God during
some desert years. He has built some godly character in
you. And regarding your airport flashback, in your quietness you spoke. My arms are for you alone.

I called my sister yesterday on flights. What are your

long-range thoughts for Christmas and New Years?

I appreciate your prayers for today. I have a couple meetings with pastors, sending out my newsletters, and three games tonight, all with my mind and heart in the Colorado Rockies.

Dreamy,

Randy

Subject: Satisfy Us O Lord
Date: 11/15

Hello, Mr. Dreamy.

I lit a special California candle last night and was thinking of you.

Much happened last night, and I'm not sure how to capture it all. First, thanks for the comments from the girls. That was nice to hear. You can tell them too that I was duly impressed . . . their welcoming hearts, smiles, genuineness. I can tell they love you lots. You all have been through a lot together. Thanks for their e-mail addresses.

Of course I will pray for you today, you are in my heart. So, you have pastors, newsletters and basketball—why don't you get the pastors to stuff your newsletters during the basketball game and talk to them at halftime?

Thanks too for your e-mail yesterday sharing some of what God spoke. I re-read it again late last night and it got to me. In fact, God used it to open me up to a time of breaking me too. I can't adequately capture it, but here is the gist.

First, that God would use me in such a way in your life touched me. He opened my heart and I began weeping at all that He has done to bring me to such a time and place. That He would honor my desire to be used by Him rendered heartfelt praise.

Then later I felt like my heart was being ripped. It had to do with Susie. I realized that I have taken on such a burden for her, with a desire and promise to be there for her. But I did not know how to do that AND keep moving closer to you with my heart and soul.

I knew that God was asking me to bring it all to His feet again. I surrendered Susie to the Lord. I released it all knowing that only Jesus can save her from this nasty cancer. I asked Him to teach me His path for me now with her. I realized anew that Susie is not mine, but His. Somehow I knew that He is taking her down another path that will be very difficult, and that I will have a part of it, but to entrust it to Him. It was the touch of the Spirit somehow.

Then I was in Psalms. He brought me to Psalm 90:12, 14, "So teach us to number our days, that we may present to Thee a heart of wisdom . . . O satisfy us in the morning with Thy lovingkindness, that we may sing for joy and be glad all our days."

I thought the Lord was asking me to do this. So I began thinking back, thinking of the past month, and considering the future. I thought about who He has made me to be, what He wants of me, and desires He has given me. I thought about embracing change and new things and gave Him permission to do whatever He wants, knowing He will fuel it.

And I am so glad you are a part of this. Thanks for being with me. It is so new for me to even think of us being a couple. Even though several men friends have come and gone in my life, I haven't ever been a couple to the extent of major change. But it feels blessed and right with you. So now my head and heart will continue to align, and pace ahead to blend with you as He leads us. May the Lord satisfy us and grant His incredible favor.

This afternoon I am taking Susie to her surgeon in Denver. She also meets with her lawyers in terms of her divorce.

You are a wonder to me, and a joy. We are both such passionate people. Funny how attractive that is.

Your arms I gladly take.

Sandy

Subject: Thy Word is Pure
Date: 11/16

Dear Beautiful Beyond Description,

Good to hear your voice—your visit seems so long ago, but it's only been three days! I must need help. Have I told you that I miss you?

Thinking back on your emotions prior to your visit, your visit here, and now a few days removed from it, how do you capture all three of those segments in your emotions, thoughts, working of God, and guarding of heart and affections? I think it includes surrender, yielding, prayer, trust, Scripture, and green lights.

I am meditating on "Worship the Lord in the beauty of holiness." Jesus is the beauty of holiness. True inner beauty equals holiness. And "O thou whom my soul loveth." What a challenge to try to love God with my soul, which equals my mind and will and emotions. How do we do that with a human?

What was your major in college?

Thanks for caring deeply for Susie, Lucretia, and others.

I'm praying for them too. Thanks for your empathy as I was sharing my story last Saturday at Claim Jumper. God has given you grace to identify with people and their issues. You are a great listener and know how to ask clarifying questions.

Thanks for sharing your time with God too. I pray for direction in regard to Susie and your emotional capacity. It's a unique balance for dependence on the Lord and friends.

Thanks for sharing about your surrender and being open to His desires and new things. I can't imagine what it's been like for you. Many times you and your way with words is simply incredible. I desire to learn to communicate my feelings better. You are beautiful, and this is very beautiful.

Thank you, Jesus. O, Savior, precious Savior, my heart is at Thy feet.

Randy

Subject: Good Communicator
Date: 11/16

Hey Randy. Sweetie, you just made my day.

Thanks for going to get the tickets and for coming out to Colorado in a few weeks! You'll need to put on your extrovert hat because you will be meeting a lot of people that weekend!

I'll find a place for you to stay, possibly with Bobbi and Jerry. They only live minutes from me.

I took a poll at headquarters and 201 out of 201 people asked, "When is Randy moving out to Colorado?"

My major in college—Three years at Ball State for a 2-year degree in business, and two years at the University of Colorado for the completion of my bachelors in marketing. And what about you? I know you are a history major. I'm assuming you also have your masters if you taught as an adjunct professor.

And what is your illustrious past in the dating scene? Are there many women who did not meet the "Weyeneth Trio" criteria of who is a good match for Dad?

I also got the pictures you sent. Thanks! The one of us is on my desk, front and center.

My friend from my summer Russia trip, Susan, told me she prayed every day for us while I was with you in California. She is great! I'm moving into a mentor role with her via long distance that I'm looking forward to. She has a wonderful heart for God.

I'll talk with you soon.

Sandy

Subject: Pollster
Date: 11/16

Loveliness,

I had the creative juices flowing tonight while waiting for your phone call. I was supposed to work on newsletters but got sidetracked to some funny postcards headed your way... am I sending too many? Do you have time to read them? Do I have your attention yet? Do you know I exist? Will I need to send you postcards for the rest of my natural life to woo your passionate heart?

I look forward to meeting as many people as you want on my trip to Colorado to see you. Bring them on. I want to meet your friends!

Yes, I am a history major with a couple of seminary courses and Bible correspondence courses thrown in, but no masters yet. I filled the University of California Berkeley NROTC/Marine Officer Instructor billet on grace—I had a successful interview! The overriding fact that I was an usher for Berkeley games when in high school and usually seated the fans in the right seats about 35 percent of the time was my best qualification.

Regarding my past dating experience, my response is: What illustrious past in the dating scene? God kept my heart closed for ten years, not so much for the ex-wife, but for Him. I had no desire to date and no woman in church seemed to be passionate for Him alone without alternative motives and manipulation. This one person my daughters met once was a woman that I met in church after joining a Christian singles club for $18. We went out a few times, then I discovered she was a very young believer. I lasted five weeks in the singles club—what can you expect for $18? I have more stories to tell about that experience than I do dates! That scene was not for me. God knew that I needed to wait for you. What was your past dating like?

Neat news on Susan; please thank her for praying for us. Judie told me she prayed for us the entire weekend too. How many others prayed as well? The weekend was truly inspired by God and unforgettable.

Thanks for the St. Lucia postcard. When you go out for Lucretia's wedding, watch out for the weirdoes on the beach. Do you need a bodyguard or someone to carry your bags? I am good at beaches.

I have an early flight tomorrow morning, then return from my parents' on Sunday night. I will call you over the weekend and leave you messages if you are out on any dates Friday, Saturday, and Sunday. I know passionate women of God are few and hard to find.

Miss you,

Randy

Subject: A new song
Date: 11/17

My dearest Randy,

Have I noticed you? Have you captured my heart? Have you wooed me? Have you warmed my heart?

Sweetheart, you have wooed me like none other. In September when I had pulled my heart back in and was "spent," you stepped out with your heart and paved a way of enjoyment, delight, and integrity. It made me feel safe to step ahead when I was reluctant but wanting.

One of my friends called you a "Randy magnet." Steady, strong, sure. When I had little to give in the initial weeks of our rapport, you were still there, a flashing light that kept drawing me when I didn't think I had much to give. And though you did not know it at the time, God used your steadiness to gradually open my eyes while I was trying to protect my heart. Thank you!

I remember the day when you stated your interest in me. I knew it was coming and it made my heart sing. I loved your honesty then and always have. Inside I intuitively knew that this was different, special.

In the past, I have been a strong initiator in relationships, with women friends and men friends. God brought me to a point where I could not do that with you because my capacity was drained. And I never knew that that would open such a wonderful door for you. Praise Him!

After a few weeks of knowing you, I wrote in my journal one of my main questions. "Lord, is he marked by love?" I did not care so much about ministry, skills, vision, status, or success if it lacked love.

I have seen the marks of love on you. How you like to give to others. The kindness of your heart. Being a gentleman. The sacrifices for your daughters. The concern for others and their well-being. The love for God that shines from you.

I so admire your passion for Him. And I know that we have only scratched the surface of seeing the depth of that in one another. I have met many men who say much about living for our Lord Jesus, but only live for Him in a lukewarm manner, men who have not been broken by Him nor truly transformed by the depths of Him. In you I see both.

I see a heart that could be bitter from what happened to you. But I see your heart as one broken and redeemed by the Lord of All. The touch of the Master who knows your soul and is perfectly able to heal through His amazing grace and unfathomable goodness.

I see a heart that stayed the course and gave all you could to your daughters. That is a mark of godliness and righteousness and praise.

I see a man who initiates and does not stay in the common and some-times surprisingly comfortable kettle of fear. I see a man who prays and thinks and offers his heart in the likeness of his Lord and Savior.

I see a tenderness that would melt the heart of anyone. It is melting mine. I see a willingness to share who you are and what you have. Things do not have you, you have them. I see a man who loves the Word of God. Who does not just claim he does, but who feeds on it, meditates and lets the incredible words of our God fill, change, and mold him. How I love that about you.

I see a man free to walk in the Spirit too. You know that there is much more than simply Bible study. You are open to the work of the Spirit and different ways God may bring it.

I see a man committed to helping his daughters succeed and launch into their lives as best they can. I see concern that they discover who they are, who they are in Christ, and follow Him fully no matter how He calls them. I hear your concern that your girls find someone who also is a man after Him and who will be good to them. And I know too that this concern and love is the mark of a man bearing His image.

I see that you know several sides of the fence—being married and being single for awhile. That works deep things in the heart when surrendered and walking with Him. It is hard to articulate, but it knows the like-heartedness of those who have also walked the path of suffering, waiting, and wanting, and living out whatever He gives or takes.

Have you warmed my heart? Without question. It is you I want to give it to! I think of you all the time.

I had a lovely start to my day today. Time with the Lord . . . started by singing Fairest Lord Jesus, and tears came thinking of His altogether loveliness. Then the Psalms that begged to lift up our praise for His lovingkindness in the morning, and in the evening for His faithfulness. What a joyous time of doing just that. His song was radiating in my heart. How can He love us so?? It moves me to give all to Him.

Last night I missed talking to you! And sure, you can be my bodyguard any day. The beach would certainly be more fun with you there! How great that would be. I shall wear a ring on my left finger to help ward off the weirdoes. And I'll bring two beach towels so it doesn't look like I am alone. I will be wise.

I have heard of the triangle illustration regarding marriage. I know that when we are linked in God, intimacy is much sweeter. It's always work in our fallen and selfish states, but sweeter with the Radiant One.

Regarding my past dating—a few men have come and gone. Have a lot of stories to tell, but there were also long, dry periods with no one. I only seriously dated one man for five months. I knew for a while that I could not marry him, but I was trying to give it a chance. I also fell for an Air Force man after our first blind date. But it ended up not working out.

Singles groups! Not for me. I was a part of one with my church in my twenties and enjoyed it. But I struggled with not meeting like-hearted people much. One of my brothers and one good friend over the years encouraged me to join a dating service, but I could not. I knew it was not for me. And through my thirties with church singles groups—no thanks. I already knew enough dysfunctional people.

So, poet and postcard man, you have me. I'm still learning and growing into this, and I am thrilled! God has opened the doors of His goodness, and I believe He is honoring us both. Knowing you has put a new song in my heart.

Yours with mighty strong affection,

Sandy

Subject: A New Song
Date: 11/19

Dearest Sandy,

What a pleasure talking with you on Friday and Saturday from Orinda!

My heart longs to visit with you soon and look into your

beautiful eyes. It's hard to beat being with you and just enjoying your presence, whether we are talking or silent.

As I think back on the brief encounter when I first met you at the coffee machine, I guess we always have first impressions whether we want to or not. I think you were introduced to me off guard a little because you were busy doing something. You seemed a little distant, appeared to be a strong woman, and definitely a professional.

My after-first impressions: fun, creative, warm, affectionate, professional, loving, caring, others-oriented, outgoing, independently dependent on God.

After a couple of weeks of e-mailing, I really was attracted to your spirit and heart. I wanted to state my intentions because I wanted to increase the level of our friendship and know all about you. I was very impressed and really cared for you and wanted heart-to-heart fellowship. I wanted to give to you. I really didn't know how you would respond—was I blowing you out of the water? I knew God was leading me, not just emotions, so it was somewhat easy to be bold and courageous to ask you, at least over e-mail, to share some of your feelings.

I appreciate God's timing in you being exhausted and at a lower capacity, and having to trust Him and me to take the initiative. God does open all the right doors in His way and time.

I appreciate your priority focus on, "Is he marked by love?" Thank you for investing in love and hearts versus the trappings of the world.

I have seen many marks of love on you, including your love for God and people, deep relationships, graciousness, poise, confident dependence on God, and faithfulness. You obey the promptings of the Holy Spirit, honor God in your calling and profession, have empathy, servanthood, neat concern for family, worship, and are passionate about God.

Your walk matches your talk.

I so appreciate your sharing of emotions, feelings, humility, and brokenness. Your desire to know Christ intimately in all areas of life.

I have not shared deep emotions and feelings with anyone in a long time and have suppressed or internalized them way too much. I guess they have been stockpiling in my heart—kind of like a reservoir waiting to burst. The Lord has been dealing with me in this area, and it started in August with the release, followed by our time at Catalina, and others.

The feelings I have for you are virgin, new, special, deep, wonderful, pure, and God given. I have never felt this kind of love with anyone! Thank you for you.

God's blessings make it rich and make you and me rich. Praise His holy name!

Thanks for your many kind words and the time to document your feelings to me. You sure know how to release the reservoir of emotions in me. Thanks for caring so much and so deeply. You have truly melted and captured my heart. I want you to give your heart to me, and I want to give you mine.

I believe God has uniquely created us to be dependent on Him and each other. As two people grow in Him independently, they cannot but help grow together as a couple. But why is this so rare today? Why are some of the loneliest people I know married? The key is the life of Christ and constant cultivation of our relationship with the Lover of our souls.

I feel awed and honored to see God bring us to meet, communicate, visit, share, and trust each other in an amazingly short span of time. I had often wondered if God would ever work out all the details for me to meet a

godly, passionate woman, or if I should just plan my life
and ministry around being single for the rest of my life.

In you, I believe that I have. To God be all the glory.
It's the work of His hands. I stand amazed at you and His
work in you.

Thank you for all the small and large steps of obedience
that you have made unto Christ over the years and your
faithful waiting for Him, His will, His best. Thanks for
not succumbing to anything less than His perfect will. You
are truly amazing!

I am yours.

Randy

Chapter 8

An Incredible Proposal

When you've waited 39 years for a marriage proposal—the kind you want to say "yes" to—you hope it will be grand. Randy did not disappoint me.

In proposing to me, Randy wanted to honor me and to honor my parents by asking for their permission to marry me. Without having met my parents yet, and unbeknownst to me, traditional Randy mailed my parents this hand-written, untraditional, and humorous letter.

To Mr. Fred and Mrs. Pat,

How are you? My name is Clifton Weyeneth but you can call me Randy. I tryed to call you on my rotary phone but I doesn't think it reaches Indianna.

I went to the movie house and seen Meet the Parents flick but Im way nervous to meat you too. So I decide to right you. My typerighter done broke so I must right on paper. Sorry bout that. Not good impression - I no that.

Mr. Fred - I fall in love with your woman - not your woman - but I mean your daughter - Sandy. She a winner and I want her to be my soulmate and wife. Im OLD school and beleive a man should honer her old man and ask for pem permission to merry. So I right you.

You dont no me two well so heres my passed life. I do well in school. Finished ten grade and authoritys said

Marines or jail. I ain't no dummie so I joined.

Got busted twice but pinned on Sargent. Was kinda war heroe in Gulf war but inhaled a lot of oil fire fumes. Don't thenk it effected me that much. Anyhoot Im nice guy and will treet your daughter well.

So how bout it - can I have her? Please return the card to me with your ansir and well go from there. Ok?

Thank you,
Randy

PS If it helps in your decision, I know Bobby Plump.
PSS Please hurry.

Enclosed with the letter was this return postcard so my parents could indicate their response and mail it back to Randy.

Mr. Fred and Mrs. Pat - Can I marry Sandy?
Check one:
o Heck yes
o Yes
o Yes, but let's talk first
o Boilermaker yes
o Someday, maybe

After sending the letter, Randy heard nothing from my parents for a couple of weeks. He started to sweat. *"Did I offend them? Why haven't I heard anything back?"* he wondered. So he called me, told me about the letter, and read it to me. I thought the letter was hilarious and assured Randy that my parents had a good sense of humor. After talking with my dad and mom, I realized they liked the letter and were simply trying to think of something clever to reply back. They had no problems with me marrying Randy. In fact, later my mom joked, "It takes a smart man to write a dumb letter!"

I also wanted to meet Randy's parents. So for Christmas, I flew out to California to meet them. It was our third face-to-face adventure, and Randy and I were giddy in love like two teenagers. I had suspected that Randy might propose to me on this trip; actually, Randy asked me to marry him more than twenty times that week!

We went for a walk and Randy smiled, "How about spending the rest of your life with me?" For a split second my mind raced, *"Is this it? Is he asking me to marry him?"* Later we drove to Baskin-Robbins and he teased, "So what are you doing for the rest of your life?" We hiked among the magnificent redwoods at the Muir Woods National Monument, and he winked, "Hey, beautiful, wanna get hitched?" On the drive home from church he grinned, "Can I sit by you the rest of my life?"

Initially I felt emotionally tossed around by these playful proposals. I kept thinking, *"Is this it? Is this the proposal?"* Finally I relaxed and had a good time with it, realizing that these were simply his spontaneous confessions of love. I believed his real proposal would be much more involved, and was it ever!

Randy planned to fly to Colorado Springs in February for a meeting, so I arranged for him to stay with friends of mine. I also guessed he would propose for real during that week. Although I didn't know it at the time, he originally planned to do it on the castle rooftop, where we had shared such a special time of worship the week we met. However, this Southern Californian forgot about the snow in Colorado. Unbeknownst to me, Randy cancelled that plan as soon as he arrived.

The snow would not be our only obstacle. Serious sickness crashed in on me that week—infected tonsils, raw throat, fever, intense aching, and pure exhaustion. I endured sore throats frequently, so I hoped this would quickly run its course. However, after one night of severe pain and fearfully abnormal breathing, I went to the doctor. The diagnosis: mononucleosis!

I discovered I had mono just two days before Valentine's Day—the day I anticipated that Randy would officially propose. Feeling absolutely lousy, I pleaded with God, *"Lord, I don't know what to do. Randy is going to propose tomorrow, and this is one of the most important days of my life. I have to feel better! Lord, I feel awful and have so little strength. Please help me. I need you. Please help me feel better and give me strength to make it through tomorrow."*

The next day I was drugged up, but felt awake, alert, and as energetic as possible. Unbelievably, I was ready and eager for whatever Randy had in store for me.

Randy drove me to the stately castle, where I had been many times for work meetings and events. Yet this time my mind was not on anything related to work. I simply followed Randy's lead and excitedly wondered what he had planned. We walked up to the third floor and entered a beautiful suite with a lovely sitting area. Randy carried in his briefcase and asked me to sit down. Heart pounding, I knew this was it! Randy started by pulling out a card and a gift. In the card, he eloquently wrote of his appreciation of my love for God. My tears began.

Reaching into his briefcase, he pulled out another card and gift. In this one, he described how he loved my faithfulness. Then another card. And another. And another. I cried throughout. Randy gave me about ten cards, all outlining qualities he admired about me. And the thoughtful gifts matched the character quality from the card or were simply things he knew I liked. But none of these things were as tender as what came next.

To profess his love and willingness to serve me, he told me he wanted to wash my feet. This symbolized how the Lord Jesus Christ, on the night before He died, humbled Himself and washed the feet of His disciples to show them His deep love and to demonstrate that love is serving. By now I needed a box of Kleenex! Randy pulled out a bottle of water and a cloth and gently washed my feet. I was speechless.

By this time, a couple of hours had passed, probably because I cried at everything. Randy's final card culminated in new words to express his love and finished by saying he wanted to spend the rest of his life with me. The gift was a small, porcelain little girl holding a heart-shaped container. As I unwrapped it, I heard a slight rattle inside the heart-shaped container. I opened the lid, and inside gleamed a diamond ring! I managed to cry some more.

Randy bent down on one knee and said, "Sandy, I would love to have you as my wife and partner. Would you marry me and spend the rest of your life with me?"

I had dreamed of enthusiastically shouting, "Yes!" at this point and jumping into his arms. But after hours of crying, my "yes" came more quietly between sobs of joy.

After embracing and crying together, we walked hand-in-hand across the room to look out the balcony. Opening the ornate glass patio door, we stepped onto the balcony and wrote our names in the snow like two school kids! This would have been the perfect time for a kiss, but of course I had mono. Still, it was one of the most romantic days of my life!

Chapter 9

Life After I Do

My first year of marriage was one of the hardest years of my life. While I never doubted my decision to marry Randy and remained thankful for the blessed way God brought us together, the major stress in transitioning to a completely new life took its toll. It felt like the rug had been yanked out from under me as absolutely everything in my life changed at once. Many of the major stress factors of life bombarded me simultaneously. In addition to getting to know Randy better and learning to be a wife, I had left my home, my friends, my job, and my identity in Colorado when I joined Randy in California. I also was suddenly a stepmom to three college-aged daughters, two of whom lived with us. Initially I felt like a stranger, an outsider, in this family that suddenly became my family. Dad and daughters had established relationships with one another; I had not. They knew the family dynamics; I did not.

Another huge adjustment was seeing that Randy was not just "mine." He was a father, loving and involved with helping his girls in this transition phase of their lives. I already knew and appreciated that, and I was willing to share in that with him. However, experiencing it firsthand felt different. I needed to temporarily lay aside some of what I looked forward to as newlyweds—special dinners for two and romantic evenings cuddled on the couch watching a movie together. Thankfully, Randy made sure I never felt second rate to his daughters. Randy cherished and loved all of us. He respected me as an equal partner and involved me in our family decisions, but it took me some time to figure out my place.

Then there was sex. As a virgin when we married, I felt nervous and unsure about the how-to's of sex. I felt pressure to perform well, and I was afraid of failing. At first, it felt awkward to suddenly undress in front of Randy. The habit of protecting and covering my body for years did not simply vanish overnight! I had to keep repeating, *"It's okay. We're married now. Yesterday it was wrong to jump in bed together, but from now on, it's okay."* That was weird. (Though I have to add that the learning curve for sexual intimacy and fulfillment created a profound bond between my husband and me.)

There were also small things that added up: Where was the grocery store? The bank? When was my new family used to having dinner? What kinds of food did they eat? Who did the household chores? Where would we go to church?

I cried randomly, without warning and without being able to explain why. Even though this was my new home and new life, several times I woke up thinking, *"How did I get here?"* Many times I felt vulnerable and overwhelmed and longed for the familiar. Never did I doubt that marrying Randy was of God, but because everything familiar to me was gone, I wasn't even sure who I was anymore.

The Lord was changing me. It was painful, yet it forged a wonderful interdependence with my husband. We both had a deep appreciation for being together (finally!) and no longer living alone. And because we were older, we both brought a cache of life and relational skills. Even with these, we encountered surprises and challenges after marriage.

After several months, during some time with the Lord, the Holy Spirit brought Lot's wife to mind. I knew the story in Genesis 19. God had declared destruction on Sodom and Gomorrah because of their wickedness and complete corruption. Two angels had come to see how bad the situation was and to rescue Lot, his wife, and their family. Lot was reluctant, but the angels grabbed him by the hand and led him and his family out, telling them to flee immediately for their lives and to not look back. But when they paused for a moment, Lot's wife looked back. Maybe at that moment she longed for the life and city so familiar to her. Instantly she died, becoming a pillar of salt.

"Lord," I asked, *"Why are you reminding me of her?"* His rebuke to me seemed harsh. All I was doing was missing my friends and what I was used to. All of this change was so hard. Yet here He was telling me to stop looking back?

That picture of Lot's wife looking back stuck in my mind. How easy it is to long for what is familiar and even feel righteous and justified in wanting it more than my current reality. That realization stung. The Lord wanted me to give it all up, to die to my longing for the familiar and surrender it to Him. In tears and obedience, I did.

The surprise was that in so doing, a new door opened! Surrendering it to the Lord birthed a peace and joy and ability to embrace the new calling of my married life and all that He had for me now. Things were still hard, but I moved forward with new perspective and peace.

A few of my bigger struggles I share with you here. They were hard at the time and in some ways still are, but in the context of a loving and trusting relationship with my husband and my complete surrender to God, these struggles became opportunities to see the Lord work in powerful ways in me.

Work and Money

For most of my life I worked a defined office job. Now I worked from home—partnering with Randy in our ministry to military men and women—with little inherent structure. Without the practical office work and do-lists I was used to, personal insecurities surfaced. What if I wasn't good at building into people? How would I start? What would accomplishment look like? Randy and I had different work styles, which were complementary at times and frustrating at others.

Initially I felt intimidated and a little insecure meeting with military wives and a few active-duty women Marines. *"I've never lived the military lifestyle, so how can I minister to these women?"* I questioned.

Many of these young women were also mothers, and I was not. But I thought, *"Okay, Lord, You have brought me here. I don't know about the military lifestyle, but I know how to be a friend. I can give these women who I am and trust You to use that."* With that, I stepped out in faith, and God met me in my willingness. What a tremendous blessing it became. The women I helped grew spiritually, and so did I!

Since the funds supporting our joint ministry work now came into one account under my husband's name, I no longer received a paycheck of my own. He was legally the official employee and suddenly I was now just the spouse. I realized that much of my self-worth had come from earning a paycheck. God reaffirmed that my worth was in Him, not in payment for my work. Nonetheless, part of me felt less valued. It took a while to get used to.

After working, getting paid, and managing my own funds for many years, I was no longer in control of my own finances. That was hard. I struggled with feeling I had to earn my keep. It did not come naturally to suddenly think that Randy's income was now my livelihood.

Randy completely opened up his finances as *our* finances. He communicated clearly and genuinely that it was all mine too. Completely trusting Randy, I could accept this, but I still struggled with feeling dependent. It took me a while to be comfortable with that, even though I accepted it intellectually as good and right.

I also opened up my small amount of savings to Randy. We talked about the desires and purposes for our money and savings, and we agreed to leave these savings designated for the purposes I had already chosen.

Children

The area of having children has been an altar of sacrifice and death many times over for me. Yet the Lord has also given grace.

In the third year of our marriage—I was 42 and Randy was 52—I got some of the best news of my life. I was pregnant! We were ecstatic.

However, it only lasted a few weeks. I miscarried shortly afterward. That loss proved one of the most painful disappointments I have ever experienced. For two decades I had hoped, prayed, faithfully walked with the Lord, and longed for the day I could have children. *"God, why did you take this baby? You have constantly affirmed me in wanting children, so why this? Is it some kind of punishment?"* I felt depressed, withdrawn, angry, and alone.

We continued to try to get pregnant again. The military hospital turned me down as a candidate for fertility treatment, saying I was too old. Month after month, we kept praying and trying to conceive with no results.

Next I brought up the idea of adopting. Randy and I talked about it and agreed to research a couple of adoption agencies. Mentally and emotionally, I already had a child in my arms! However, the further we got into the process, the less Randy was convinced. Eventually, after much prayer and some godly counsel, he lacked the peace of God and said he did not want to adopt. I was livid. *"I thought he agreed to adopting, so how could he say this now? Why was he open to having children naturally but not to adopting?"* For me, having children naturally and adopting were almost the same—God providing children, just through different means. It had never occurred to me that Randy might not want to adopt.

A crisis of faith hit me. In this heart-wrenching pain, Satan tempted me to believe a brutal lie, questioning if I had married the right man. The insipid insinuation was that if I had married someone else, I could have had children.

Deep down, I realized my core issue was not my anger at my husband. I felt betrayed by God. Why couldn't God allow me to conceive again or make my husband say yes to adoption?

Then I got an almost prophetic glimpse of how easy it is to become bitter, to hang on to anger and feel justified in wanting to hurt or punish someone for causing your pain. Bitter people remain angry. They push away other people and God. I did not want to be bitter. Inside I felt ripped apart because I also knew that I loved my husband. Walking into our bedroom, I shut the door, knelt down and prayed with tears.

"Lord, I believe in You and affirm my faith in You. You are God and there is no other. You are holy and good and altogether righteous. Your Word and your promises are true. I love You and choose to follow You even though I can't understand all of this and my heart is broken. I know that You gave Randy to me and affirm that he is a gift from You. Our marriage is a gift from You. Thank You for that and for all You did to bring us together. I do love Randy even though this is so hard right now. Randy is not my enemy. He loves me and is for me. Thank You for calling us together for Your purposes.

"Lord, I hurt so much I don't know what to do. I am so angry. I know that You love me, but I feel like You have let me down. You have always affirmed my desire for children. You know how much I have wanted children. I have waited on You and stayed true and faithful, and now that I am married and have the opportunity to have children, I can't. I know that You could change Randy's heart regarding adoption if You wanted to.

"But Lord, he does not want to adopt. And I know that to go ahead with adopting, we must be in complete agreement, so I surrender this to You. I give You my womb to do as You see fit. I surrender my desire for adoption as well. I don't know what to do, but please show me. Lead us as You always have. I love You and bless Your name."

God changed me that day. Today it is a miracle to me that I am not still mad at my husband. I only know that when we completely surrender to Jesus, somehow He takes out the thorn.

Since then, I carry a sorrow that I believe will remain until I am in heaven with Jesus. Certain situations and conversations prick that tender spot. But I choose not to dwell there. Instead, I lift my eyes to the Savior who bled on a cross for me. And I choose gratefulness for the brief joy of having known life inside of me.

Also, a few years later I came to understand a couple of significant things that I had not known at that time. First, Randy did not share my thinking that having children and adopting were "almost the same." To him, adopting was a very different ball game. Second, Randy was torn up about this decision. Because of his love for me, he wanted to please me. Yet he had to be true to how he believed God was leading as well.

Why having children was not part of God's plan for me, I have no idea. But I know He knows. His purposes are ultimately good and far above mine. I know He loves me. I know that He is honored when we obey Him and live the life He has for us. And I will praise Him for all that He is.

Living as Newlyweds

Randy and I decided that we would stay newlyweds forever. That means that we work to cherish one another. (Yes! Sometimes it takes work!) We keep going on dates and continue doing little extra things to express our affection. After a few years of marriage, it's easy to take one another for granted. We grow increasingly annoyed by our differences and personal issues. Frustration mounts from having to keep working through conflicts and disagreements. It takes work to engage from the heart, to forgive one another, and to address real issues without nagging or demanding. It takes effort to express gratitude. By choosing to live as newlyweds, we are intentionally doing the hard work to keep our relationship fresh and growing and enjoyable.

Do I miss being single? Okay, I'll admit there are a few things: having more spontaneity with my schedule, occasionally cleaning house at 10:00 p.m., and getting to pick whatever movie I'd like. (I've watched a few more action and war movies than I care for since marrying Randy!) Strange as it may sound, I also miss the unique and sweet aspect of undistracted devotion to the Lord. When it was just me and Jesus, so to speak, that dependency and availability to the Lord forged a gratifying and special sense of intimacy with Him.

Looking back over my single years, over how God brought me love worth the wait and now as a wife, I'm reminded of a few important truths. Frequently, "the grass seems greener" on the other side. In other words, when struggles and challenges come, something else often looks more appealing than our current reality. However, God desires that instead of continually gazing at the "greener grass," we gaze at Him. Single or married, He longs for us to find our soul contentment, purpose, and joy *in Christ*. As we do, He enables us to carry genuine longings in our heart for love and relationship and gives us grace to wait on Him.

In marriage, I am called to wait on God as well. It reflects dependency and trust in Him. It also allows God to work in ways that only He can. My husband is fond of quoting Hudson Taylor's wise observation: "God's will, done in God's way, in God's time, will never lack God's supply." What a beautiful description of trust and dependency. Isaiah 40:31 promises that those who wait for the LORD will gain new strength. Psalm 27:14 (NASB) also directs us to "Wait for the LORD; be strong, and let your heart take courage; yes, wait for the LORD." Waiting for the Lord God means to expect, look for, and hope in Him.

As you wait on the Lord of all creation, the second part of this book offers some practical tips and wisdom to help and encourage you in this journey. These will help you enjoy a sweeter walk with Jesus, lead a spiritually fruitful life, and make a difference for eternity.

Part 2

Behind the Scenes:
Proven Principles
to Find Your Love Story

Chapter 10

Is This "The One"?

Shawna had dated Justin for a couple of years when he proposed. Elated, she said yes. They were engaged for two years while Justin finished college. Shawna believed she knew Justin very well and thought she was in love with him. However, during their engagement, she began to have nagging doubts. Although Justin was a believer in Christ and a nice man, he was not genuinely pursuing the Lord on his own. A friend shared his observation with Shawna—that life for Justin seemed to be more about Justin than it was about serving the Lord. With greater clarity, Shawna admitted that she and Justin were not on the same footing spiritually, and that she wanted and needed more of that. With great courage, she called off the engagement.

Some sadness and tears followed, but Shawna experienced greater peace, freedom, and relief after honestly telling Justin she could not marry him and why. It scared her how close she had come to spiritually compromising just because it felt so good to "have someone." Shawna wanted to focus on growing in her relationship with the Lord, much like 1 Corinthians 7:35 describes as "undivided devotion to the Lord." She went on with her life, trusting that if the Lord wants her to marry, He will bring the right man along at the right time.

The reality of being hitched together for the rest of your life, day in and day out, deserves honest and serious attention. Your time spent dating and even your engagement period are opportunities to learn about someone at a deep level and see if your lives are genuinely compatible. The author of the book *Brown Like Coffee* states that most married couples are shocked when they realize that 90 percent of their dating period was filled with activities and only 10 percent communication. After the honeymoon, those percentages reverse themselves!

Although falling in love is easy to do, feelings alone are not enough to bear the weight of such a huge commitment. That's because feelings change. While feelings are a vital aspect of relationship, the foundation of marriage must be built on something more solid than feelings. Intimately walking with Jesus, and living as He taught us to live, is the more solid foundation. So as you wonder if this person you are dating is the one for you, communicate well, observe character well, listen well, and seek the Lord about His will for this relationship.

My husband aptly says that marriage is not primarily meant to make us happy, but to make us holy. When we believe 2 Corinthians 5:14–15 (NASB), it will overhaul our perspective on marriage: "For the love of Christ controls us . . . and He died for all, that they who live should no longer live for themselves, but for Him who died and rose again on their behalf." As we first seek God and His holiness (to be like Jesus and live for others instead of just wanting what will make me happy), that radically shifts our self-centeredness to others-centeredness. As we first seek God and His holiness, it's hard to contain the joy and happiness that God floods into our lives and marriage. While dating, observe if your partner is primarily living for himself, or if he is willing to serve others. Is the love of Christ influencing him or her to that degree?

You also want to take your time during your courtship. This is not something you want to rush! This is one of the biggest decisions you will ever make, and it will deeply impact the rest of your life—for better or for worse! Randy and I fell in love at turbo speed after only a couple of months. Because we were both older and had walked with God for many years, we had a better understanding of real relationship and were more discerning of the kind of character we were looking for in a mate. Despite our unique situation, a good rule of thumb is to date for at least a year to decide if this is the person you should marry.

That may seem like a long time when you're in love and anxious to get on with your life together, but this period of "due diligence" will definitely pay off in the long run. Instead of just hanging out and having fun together, be around one another in a variety of normal life situations as well—grocery shopping, a basketball game, doing laundry, or a road trip.

While dating Randy, I felt thrilled and scared, telling my friend Shireen, "I like this, but it is going so fast!" I wanted to slow it down because my iron-clad ideal for dating included plenty of time to observe a man's personality, character, values, and the substance of his life. Shireen grinned and replied, "I know. I've been praying that it would go fast for you." Great!

Occasionally, crazy, out-of-the-blue thoughts assaulted my mind. Flashbacks of *America's Most Wanted* popped into my head—you know, where the wife discovers her husband leads a double life and is really a convicted felon on the run! Nervously I worried, *"How well do I really know this man I'm dating?"*

An emotional circus played out inside my mind. The more I saw and heard from Randy, the stronger the pull toward him. But my rational side fueled the push to keep some distance and keep my heart in check. After all, I hardly knew him, had spent little time with him, and yet here I was falling in love with him!

Feeling loved and beautifully pursued by this wonderful man felt delicious and breathtaking. Wasn't it a no-brainer to marry this man I was in love with and whose character I so admired?

When Randy invited me out to meet his parents and siblings over Christmas, I suspected that he might propose during the trip. Wanting to be ready and to be assured that God was leading me to marry Randy, I spent a couple of extended periods of time with the Lord. God promises that He will lead, direct, and counsel us as we seek Him and His will. The following questions helped me think and pray through whether Randy was "the one" for me.

QUESTIONS TO DISCERN GOD'S WILL FOR MARRIAGE

1. What is God telling you from His Word?

Have you earnestly asked the Lord for clear direction from His Word and committed to follow it—whether it's the answer you're looking for or not? Our Creator, the God of the universe, delights in leading us personally and giving us relevant principles and truths from His Word. In times past, as I sought God and spent time in His Word, the Spirit impressed a particular verse or two that spoke directly to me. As I reviewed those scriptural promises, I saw that marrying Randy was in line with each one.

In addition, after thinking, praying, and quietly listening to the Lord one night, I had an overwhelming sense from the Holy Spirit, resounding in one word: "Behold." It was as clear as if God audibly spoke it to me. *"Sandy,* behold *what I have done. This is of My hand and it is for you. Take it."*

2. What do trusted friends and family members think of the relationship?

Often the people who know us best can see things we may be blind to or may be denying. They can also provide astute input and observations and help us think objectively.

3. Are you ready to accept the responsibilities of marriage?

Some nervousness is natural in making such a total and permanent commitment. But if you detect anything more than superficial jitters, bring these before the Lord and examine them closely. Be honest with yourself about any misgivings and take them seriously. Maybe this is the right person but the wrong time. Marriage is hard work, and perhaps one of you isn't ready for it yet. Or maybe it's just the wrong person and you need to find the strength and courage to end the relationship. There's no better time than now to do it.

I had peace about making the commitment to love and serve Randy for the rest of my life. I was willing to accept the responsibilities as well as the privileges of being married.

4. Is your potential spouse committed to a real, growing relationship with Christ?

Is knowing God and walking closely with the Lord the number-one love and passion in this person's life, apart from you or anyone or anything else? Has he or she learned to submit to the authority of Christ? Do you see evidence of growth? If you are the one usually bringing up spiritual issues or forcing Bible study and church attendance, pull back and allow the other person to initiate spiritually. If that doesn't happen, you'll have a good heart indicator and a good idea of what will happen after you're married.

5. Do you see Christ-like character, shared values, and similar life direction in this person?

In other words, does marrying this person fit God's present agenda for your life?

Christ-like Character—Author Leslie Ludy identifies two common tendencies for women: perfection and desperation. While most of us have a mental list of qualities we want in a man, the problem comes when we take that list to an extreme and expect perfection. Jesus Christ was the only perfect person, and outside of Him, perfection does not exist. Keep high standards about the kind of character you're looking for, Christ-like character, but do not expect perfection.

Another tendency for women is becoming desperate. Desperation comes when we are so hungry for attention and affection that we settle for guys who simply do not know how to treat a woman. In my younger years, this was true of me. We fail to trust or even believe that God may have something better for us. Ludy concludes,

"Maybe my childhood imaginations [for a husband] had been a bit larger than life. But in no way did God want me to settle for one of the typical 'jerks' who were a dime-a-dozen. He wanted me to save myself for a man who had His very nature and character within him. And He wanted me to trust Him enough to bring that special man to me in His perfect time. Guess what? In His perfect time, that's exactly what He did. Eric is my gorgeous and gallant knight in shining armor. I am so glad I didn't settle for second best."[3]

Here are several questions to get you thinking about realistic Christ-like character:

QUESTIONS TO DISCERN TRUE CHARACTER

- Is this someone I really trust? Do I see integrity and commitment to following through on promises?
- Does this person honestly enjoy me, or is he/she just out for something?
- Is there a willingness to take risks for the sake of love, such as full disclosure and being honest about intentions?
- Has this person learned to be in control of his/her sexuality?
- Is this person secure in his/her God-given identity?
- Are selflessness and giving part of this person's lifestyle?

Values—Randy and I share the same core values, primarily a love for God and living for His kingdom purposes. We also both value faithfulness, integrity, purity, communication, hard work, and handling money wisely. Take time to talk about your values and find out how similar they are. If one or two important values do not line up, then think seriously about that. It's easy to convince yourself you can live with it or to believe that your love will change this person. Don't count on that. You may be asking for heartache. One man was in love with a friend of mine, but he lacked control over his finances and often overspent. It was a big enough difference in values that she broke off the relationship.

Direction—As much as possible, you both want to be headed in a similar general direction in life. Randy and I, for example, both felt called to ministry and to giving our lives to eternal things. Do you know your potential spouse's vocational direction and aspirations? How does that line up with how God is leading you? If you are called to be a pastor and your girlfriend wants no part of that life, it would be unwise to marry her right now. If one of you wants children and the other does not, do not marry. If you don't want the same things out of life and are not headed in the same general direction, you will reap heartache. Be willing to wait for God's best for you. His timing is perfect!

6. Are you physically attracted to this person and satisfied with how he/she takes care of himself/herself?
You should have some kind of acceptance and compatibility in terms of age, health, physical features, and level of fitness.

7. What about other important circumstances and issues?
Several other factors can also be significant. Here are a few examples:

Providing—Many women long to be cared for and provided for. If this is important to you, does this man accept the responsibility and demonstrate a strong desire and willingness to provide financially for his family? (This is an important aspect of God's design for manhood.)

Debt—Does one of you carry significantly more debt that the other? How was this debt incurred? How will it affect your marriage? Randy was not in financial debt, which I highly valued. I also had no debt, except for a house mortgage.

Past—Are you comfortable with the issues from his or her past? Has there been full disclosure? Because Randy was divorced, I needed to be sure that this relationship and related issues were resolved before I would agree to marry him. What I learned assured me that it was resolved and that it had been a biblical divorce for him.

Children—Have you talked about having children, what kind of parents you want to be, and how many kids you'd like to have? You should even talk about how you will respond if you are not able to have children. This was an essential question for Randy and me. If he had not been willing to have more children, I would not have continued in the relationship.

Sense of Humor—Do you laugh at and enjoy the same things? Randy and I clicked almost instantly because of our similar sense of humor, and it continues to add spice to our lives!

Hobbies and Interests—Do you share a few hobbies or interests? In the busy years ahead, you'll need to look for ways to spend time together, and common interests make that much easier. While individual interests are healthy and important, if they take priority over spending time together now, this will surely be the case once you're married. Identify the things you like to do together. Randy and I like to take walks, people-watch, enjoy scenic spots, take historic tours, and ride our bicycles.

8. Do you have your parents' blessing and counsel?
If you trust your parents and value their opinion, you'll want to be sure they support your decision. In *Believing God for His Best*, Bill

Thrasher shares this story:

> *"The bride and groom are ultimately responsible to make their decision before the Lord. While on one extreme it might be unwise to marry someone for the sole purpose of satisfying one's parents, it would be equally unwise not to honor them by carefully weighing their advice and cautions.*
>
> *Yesterday I talked to one dear young man who waited one year for his parents-in-law's blessing. The reason that it was being withheld was his career path. He desired to follow God's call to be a pastor, but the father of the girl desired him to come work in his business and receive a lucrative salary. As he observed the genuine character of the young man for over a year, he gave his blessing for them to be married. Such a wait was helpful in his relationship with his father-in-law, who began to open his heart to spiritual truth. It also was a great relief for his wife to enter the marriage under the blessings of both her parents."*[4]

After working through these considerations and adding them all up, I knew Randy was the one for me. I encourage you to do the same and to give each one the time and attention they require. In Appendix C and Appendix D, you'll find more questions and information to help you think through your relationship and this life-altering decision.

MAKE IT REAL

- How do you seek to honor the Lord and the other person in a relationship?
- How do women help or hinder our brothers in Christ to be the men God calls them to be—initiators and pursuers in dating and courtship?
- If you are dating, what are you learning about yourself? About the person you are dating? About your relationship?

Chapter 11

The Power of a Kiss

I would love to see the kiss restored to a high and honorable place. A kiss should be intensely personal. It should follow falling in love, not be a prerequisite to it. What is so special about a kiss if you just kiss anyone you date? Men especially tend to view kissing as more recreational, missing the essence of real relationship and integrity. God calls men to treat women as sisters, with absolute purity (1 Timothy 5:2), which *does not* include recreational kissing.

Kissing should be beautiful and sacred, something worth reserving for the person you will spend your life with. Kissing on television and in movies today glorifies the passion but has little to do with committed love. Old movies, however, often show a relationship building before there's any kissing. I like that. They show real relationship growing through what the main characters say and do and through the quality of their character. It used to be understood that real relationship is primarily of the heart, not the lips. The remake of the movie *Pride and Prejudice* demonstrates love and romance superbly. Miss Elizabeth and Mr. Darcy do not start off attracted to one another, but when their lives become intertwined, Mr. Darcy sees Elizabeth's character and heart. Eventually she also sees that his integrity is far greater than she initially presumed. Without any kissing, he shows his interest in her. The consummate gentleman, Mr. Darcy also seeks to make amends in meaningful ways for a mistake he made. Elizabeth's heart melts. You see, anyone can kiss, but who can love?

The foundation of real love, as God designed it, is to include serving and self-control. It includes a commitment to being faithful to just one person. Character and integrity are at its core. For this reason, we are to make every effort to live as 2 Peter 1:5–7 (NASB) instructs: "In your faith supply moral excellence, and in your moral excellence, knowledge; and in your knowledge, self-control, and in your self-control, perseverance, and in your perseverance, godliness; and in your godliness, brotherly kindness, and in your brotherly kindness, Christian love." This progression starts with "moral excellence"—character.

Kissing is certainly a glorious part of love between a man and woman, and it helps to think of it more as an "I do" type of celebration. When a man kisses a woman on the lips, he should first know that he has chosen her to be his wife and is committed to marrying her. The kiss should come after his sincere verbal declaration of his love for her. That shows respect and honor.

Also, if you are dating someone and decide to break it off, it will be much easier if you have not kissed.

Because Randy and I dated long distance, when we were at last face to face, we wanted to physically express our admiration and affection. Yet because of our respect for each another, we decided to wait. Our urges and desires were no different from anyone else's, and it certainly wasn't easy, but I committed to not kiss Randy until he had first declared his love for me. The weekend he told me he loved me was incredibly special. It was during my visit over Christmas, and it was made even more meaningful by our first kiss. Because Randy had declared his love and I was confident his marriage proposal would follow, I was able to kiss him with complete trust.

Too many couples spend much more time being physically intimate than truly getting to know one another and learning how to communicate. Kissing and getting to know a person's body have nothing to do with getting to know the core of a person and who they really are. Don't believe the message that kissing is harmless fun. It is an intimate, personal connection with another person. It's also the gateway to even greater physical intimacy, which we'll look at in the next chapter.

MAKE IT REAL

- How can holding off on kissing while dating help build the type of affection and loyalty you long for? What does that type of self-control reveal about someone's character?

- When a man holds off kissing you on the lips until he is certain of his love and desire to marry you, how does that demonstrate respect for you? Why is mutual respect foundational for committed love?

- How can waiting to kiss strengthen the quality of a dating relationship? What are some ways that kissing early on in a relationship can "muddy the waters" or become a substitute for real rapport?

Chapter 12

The Fabulous and Freeing Pure Lifestyle

Of all the gifts I could give to Randy, the best one was intensely personal. I was a virgin when we married.

My commitment to honor God included a decision to put off sex until I was married. I stayed sexually pure for 39 years and have no regrets. Because I reserved my sexuality for my husband only, I brought no guilt or haunting flashbacks into our marriage. I brought no regrets or sexually transmitted diseases. You see, there are things worth giving up for a time so that they can be more perfectly experienced later on.

It's not that I was never tempted. I longed to be loved. A few times I made poor choices. My desire to kiss and be held by a man felt overwhelming at times. Like anyone, I was well aware of the world's lure to live for the moment and indulge in the sensual. But in the end, these leave a trail of guilt, shame, and feeling used. I knew they were not the basis of real love—or even romance, for that matter. Romance is not a matter of hormones or physical pleasure; it's a matter of the head and the heart. Speaker and author Joni Eareckson Tada, a quadriplegic for more than three decades, surprised talk-show host Larry King by explaining this to him. When King asked a personal question that indicated his disbelief that a marriage could be fulfilling without sex, Joni replied, "Oh, Larry, don't you understand that romance is from the neck up?"

Lies About Sex

We've all heard the world's tireless and pervasive lies about sex. That you can have wonderful, commitment-free sex with anyone. That you have to give sex to keep a man's love. Or that you're just plain weird without sex. Or that if you postpone sex until marriage you are somehow ridiculous or boring or out of touch. Many use this analogy referring to sex, "Who buys shoes without trying them on first?" Nothing could be further from the truth!

Too many people think that you are not a real man or a real woman until you have had sex. However, that assumes that sex is a rite of passage, that somehow sex proves your maleness or femaleness. That is a distorted and false assumption. Sexual performance was never intended to prove our worth or our personhood. There is tremendous dignity given to men and women already because God created us in His image. We also see in Scripture that what makes you a man or woman can be summed up in a word—maturity. The DNA of biblical maturity includes moral excellence, restraint, and self-control, all for the sake of love. If being a real man resulted from having sex, then you would have to believe that Jesus was not a real man. That's absurd. Jesus was a real man and our perfect example of mature, godly character.

God gave sexual intimacy as a gift to a husband and wife. He created it as a pleasurable and holy union for marriage. Because there is enormous sexual freedom, joy, and pleasure within marriage, God drew a fence around that relationship. By limiting sex to the union of marriage, God is not trying to rob us of fun. He's trying to protect us physically and emotionally. It's His gentleness and kindness that are behind His command for sexual purity.

Veteran missionary and author Elisabeth Elliot received the following letter from a woman who pleaded for her story to be passed along to others:

"At seventeen years of age I chose to rebel against God and entered a relationship with my boyfriend that delivered not happiness but guilt and grief. I 'fell in love' and rather than trust God, I went after the object of my desire with all the wiles and passions of a teenage romantic. At first what we did 'felt good'—for the moment. I tried pushing my guilt into a closet and shutting the door, but kept on doing what came naturally. I remember thinking even then, 'What will you say to your daughter someday if she asks, "Were you a virgin when you got married?" ' Over the years that question has come to mind time and time again.

That day before the wedding my fiancé forced himself on me, and never having said no before, I felt helpless to stop him. All these years later I still feel the hurt and violation of that moment. There was no tenderness, no love, only desire, lust, passion.

How could I have known the repercussions through the years of that one decision on my part to have my own way and not God's? I realize what a precious, holy gift we so thoughtlessly threw away in our youth. And now I have had to ask my daughter, 'Are you pregnant?' and hear her tearful reply, 'Yes.' I cannot express in words the deep wound to my soul this has caused. Although I did not make her decisions for her, I see that by my actions and choices so many years ago, I left her spiritually vulnerable to Satan's onslaught.

If only I could look each teenage girl in the eye and tell her, 'There are consequences to every moral decision you make; there are repercussions that will follow you the rest of your life and into the next generation!'

How I yearn to look each teenage boy in the eye and tell him, 'Be strong. Be a real man. Trust God's Word, discipline yourself, don't give in to youthful lust and trade your birthright of godly love for a mess of pottage that will turn to ashes in your heart.'

I have learned too late the truth I heard a man of God say: 'Love can always wait to give. Lust can never wait to get.'

And you know—it's funny, not a single time did those solemn moments of passion and lust bring real pleasure to me, either physically or emotionally."[5]

Giving yourself sexually to someone before marriage steals part of your heart, and you can never get it back. Sexual union is not simply a physical act; it is a spiritual act created to form a spiritual bond between a husband and wife. Sex is powerful! God designed it to be like permanent glue. Used properly, sex has awesome potential for good. Used improperly, the good is destroyed.

The anonymous author of *Brown Like Coffee* says:

"I believe sexual sins leave the deepest scars in people's lives. We can be forgiven of any evil doing, but, for some reason, it's almost impossible for us to forget these 'sins of the flesh' that seem to be seared into our conscience for many years to come. Whether it's pre-marital sexual involvement or the cheap substitutes we find in a lot of TV, movies and romance novels, they rob us of our purity, self esteem, and worst of all—fellowship with the Lord."[6]

Why Wait?

Maybe you've been in a sexual relationship and miss it. Or maybe you have been single for years like I was and you don't know if you'll ever get the chance to experience it. Remember one thing: We choose sexual purity first and foremost for our Lord Jesus Christ because He is worthy. Pleasing Him is what matters!

Sex is something He takes very seriously. If you violate God's will and have sex outside of marriage, it is sin, and it comes with consequences. You also grieve your heavenly Father who wants the best for you. God revealed His will for us: "Let marriage be held in honor among all, and let the marriage bed [sexual union] be undefiled; for fornicators [sex between unmarried persons] and adulterers [sex with someone who is married] God will judge" (Hebrews 13:4, NASB).

In his book, *Boy Meets Girl*, Joshua Harris talks about moments of sexual temptation when we have to choose between what our bodies crave and what we know our Lord has instructed.

"Will you heed the clear commands of Scripture and the

voice of your conscience, or the voice of compromise that's offering immediate pleasure? What's *really* going to make you happy? We all know how we're supposed to answer, but when our desire kicks in, doing what's right isn't easy. In the heat of passion, we need more than just knowledge about sexual purity. To stand firm against sin, we can't simply intellectually agree with the merits of chastity. We must be captivated by the beauty and greater pleasure of God's way. This involves agreeing with God about the goodness of pure sex within marriage, refusing the counterfeits offered by the world, and fearing the consequences of illicit sex."[7]

He adds, "While we're single or in a courtship, we need to do more than just avoid what's wrong—we need to plan and work hard at being captivated by the good."[8]

God wisely warns us not to flirt with physical touch and passionate kissing because He understands our bodies. He hard-wired men and women to beautifully respond to these physical triggers—triggers that easily and rightly ignite the path to sexual intercourse. That is precisely why single men and women must consciously and rightly curtail the triggers and steer away from overly-tempting situations. Song of Songs 2:7 says, "Do not arouse or awaken love until it so desires." In other words, do not stir or ignite sexual passion until you can follow through with it in marriage.

Sexual Redemption

Maybe you have already been sexually active as a single. If you have sinned sexually, the Lord Jesus Christ can and will forgive you. God longs to restore your soul. Genesis 1:27 says that God made you in His image, and He feels joy in your dignity as a human being. He will make you clean and give you a new and fresh start! That is the beauty of God in His profound grace—He gives us another chance.

Some call this a second virginity, spiritually speaking, which means choosing virginity from now on.

Derrick was having sex with his girlfriend, and he intended to propose marriage to her soon. After his Bible study leader talked with him and they looked at some Scripture together, Derrick learned that sex outside of marriage is sin against God. So he decided to obey God. He talked with his girlfriend and they agreed to stop having sex and wait for their wedding day. He confessed his sin and said, "I am so glad! I have more anticipation for our wedding day and more respect and peace of mind in obeying God."

Temptation and bad choices are common to all of us. The Lord can give you the power to forgive yourself and those who have used you. If you have not done so, confess your past sexual sin to the Lord and ask Him to forgive you. He quickly forgives a repentant heart, and as author Paula Rinehart aptly points out, nothing feels cleaner than repentance! Also, admit it to a trusted friend or family member. Their continued love will help you heal from any guilt or shame buried inside. For women, I also highly recommend Paula Rinehart's book, *Sex and the Soul of a Woman: The Reality of Love and Romance in an Age of Casual Sex*. Paula points out that there is nothing more binding to your soul than unforgiveness, and she offers a prayer you can use to help you forgive any man who may have mistreated you:

In the name of Jesus and by the power that raised him from the dead, I ask you, Lord, to sever whatever negative spiritual and emotional ties were created in the promiscuity of this relationship.

I confess and renounce my sin and the idolatry of preferring any love over yours.

I ask you to speak truth to the deepest part of me, and I renounce the lie (name the lie) I believed as a result of this experience. Knowing your willingness to forgive me, I offer this same forgiveness to the man/men with whom I have been involved.

I ask your Spirit to cleanse me from every promiscuous image, every ungodly thought. Please gather up every fragment of my soul and make me whole again. Make me, above all, yours.

I praise you for your mercy, and I claim, in Jesus Christ, the freedom and power to lay hold of my destiny as a daughter of the living God.[9]

If you have had sex with someone but have kept it a secret, or if someone sinned against you by violating you sexually, please find a trusted mentor or friend or support group and bring your secret "into the light." Let others help you. The power of the risen Savior and help from friends or counselors will help you eventually feel whole again.

Unwanted sexual advances can injure our souls with shame. Years ago, when I was in high school, I naively got into a friend's car after he had been drinking. I honestly thought we would go somewhere and simply kiss a little, and at that time, I thought that's what you did when you liked someone. Instead, he turned onto an isolated dirt lane, parked the car, started kissing me, and then attempted to take my clothes off. Utterly shocked and scared, I fiercely held my coat closed and continually refused. Thankfully, he finally gave up and drove me back to my car, mocking me audaciously. For a few years afterward, shame crashed over me, and I kept that night a secret.

A few years later I was growing spiritually and realized I felt bitter and hated this young man for his attempts at sex that night. In time, I confessed it, and the Lord helped me truly forgive him. Amazingly, the guilt and bitterness dissolved. I also told a few trusted friends, and their compassion and understanding allowed me to feel loved and helped erase the shame. I was free!

Sex Within Marriage

Sexual intimacy is designed as a special, beautiful, and intensely personal bond in marriage. To protect that, purity must continue in marriage with equal tenaciousness. Immoral temptations do not vanish or necessarily decrease while married. Self-control is a fruit of the Holy Spirit and a chosen lifestyle, single and married. Thus, God Himself will help us exercise self-control and God-control. Living in moral purity always honors the Lord and adds sizzle and profound joy in sexual intimacy with your spouse.

Purity Never Just Happens

It is no surprise that moral purity never "just happens." We work at it, leaning on the total sufficiency of the Lord Jesus Christ. We either win or lose the battle for purity with every little decision we make. That is because immorality and sexual sin begin in the mind first. It's like a fast-moving river.

How does a river become powerful? Go back to the initial source and picture a snow-capped mountain. The snow slowly melts and forms small tributaries. The tributaries flow downhill and merge with other tributaries, forming a stream. Streams merge and eventually dump into a river boasting power and speed.

The raging river never began as a raging river. It started small and was fed. Immorality almost never instantly happens simply from a choice to give in to temptation. The temptation is fed. What you fill your mind with and the thoughts you entertain are like the tributaries. The more you or I allow, the more those thoughts join with other thoughts and build momentum, leading us straight to the door of sin, sometimes deadly sin. Cut off the tributaries now, and they will not become a raging river.

Making Decisions for Purity

Cutting off the tributaries involves guarding our bodies (what we do), our minds (what we think about), our eyes (what we look at), our ears (what we listen to), and our hearts (what we treasure). This path to purity brings amazing freedom, fulfillment, and fruitfulness.

So what does it look like to choose purity? Here are some examples:

- A fiction book became more sensual than expected. It enticed and caused me impure thoughts and fantasies, so I finally got rid of it.
- A country music CD I enjoyed featured a cover picture of the singer purposefully showcasing her body. I tried convincing myself that it did not matter, reasoning the singer was not a Christian and thus did not know any better. Yet I kept comparing my body to hers, and I always lost. Finally, I threw the whole CD away. It was a huge relief afterward, and, surprisingly, I did not miss the music that much!
- Pretty lingerie for my husband is special and fun, but after Victoria's Secret catalogs started arriving in my mailbox, I called three times and asked to be removed from their mailing list. This catalog was a definite stumbling block for my husband and any men or boys in my house.
- While researching information on the internet, I accidentally stumbled upon a sexually-explicit site. Shocked, I immediately got out of it.
- One godly married friend travels a lot. When staying in hotel rooms overnight by himself, he calls the front desk and tells them to block all adult channels from the television in his room.
- A rock music CD from my younger years had lyrics promoting and idolizing "free sex" and attitudes of rebellion. Initially I did not think about the lyrics that much. Eventually, I realized how degrading they were, so I got rid of it. I still enjoy some classic, good 'ole rock-n-roll and soft rock, just not the mocking or immoral stuff.
- One decent television show highlighted a fun and romantic attraction between a single man and the single woman who worked together. After the handsome man showed up in my dreams more than once, I decided that even though I enjoyed the show, it needed to go! I fasted from watching it for a while.

- One bar/restaurant where I occasionally enjoyed a meal with friends had an after-dinner band and dancing on weekends. However, the overtly sensual dancing stirred unchecked physical appetites and lust, so I never went back. There were plenty of other good restaurants to choose from!
- A stranger kept eyeing me in an airport lounge while we both waited for our flight. He was obviously flirting, and I was married, so I moved seats and avoided contact with him.
- Realizing that God designed men to be stimulated visually, I dress in a way that draws attention to my face and not other parts of my body. This serves my brothers in Christ, in the spirit of Philippians 2:3–4.

With regard to how we dress and how we behave around other Christian men, Paula Rinehart also cautions about the power of feminine influence:

"Sometimes women are conscious of being seductive—and the prize just seems to justify the chase. Especially if there's been a real lack of male attention and affection from a girl's father as she is growing up, the need to fill that absence can be enormous. And sometimes a woman is not aware of what motivates her—she hasn't connected the way she dresses or comes on to a guy with something that's harmful to them both. She just sees something she wants.

The dark side of feminine influence—seductiveness and manipulativeness—are radically altered if we are free enough to see a man first as a brother. Romans 14:13 admonishes, 'Make up your mind not to put any stumbling block or obstacle in your brother's way.' If a guy is really a brother first, then your motivation will be to do whatever honestly serves him."[10]

After making these choices, did I feel like I was missing out? No!

In fact, I felt free! Clean! Closer to the Lord. I showed more respect toward others. I like how Nancy Leigh DeMoss puts it: "When we set and keep biblical boundaries of moral purity, the blessings that result are like ripples of water from a stone thrown into a pond. It is a commitment that wonderfully and powerfully affects our own health and spiritual welfare, our relationships, our homes, and our culture."[11]

Without question, this is a radical deviation from the way of the world. This sort of God-ordained purity is what the world actually belittles. Jesus Christ was radical and His kingdom completely different. Sexual purity is part of His good and true kingdom living (1 Peter 1:15). He has made us new creations (2 Corinthians 5:17) so that we don't have to play by the world's rules anymore. God calls us to go against the grain of culture and reject a self-centered, sensual lifestyle.

God's ways are designed to make life work. First Corinthians 6:18–19 is clear: "Flee from sexual immorality. All other sins a man [or woman] commits are outside his body, but he who sins sexually sins against his own body. Do you know that your body is a temple of the Holy Spirit, who is in you, whom you have received from God? *You are not your own; you were bought at a price. Therefore honor God with your body*" (emphasis added). We honor and love Jesus when we humbly do what He says.

MAKE IT REAL

- Spend a few minutes thinking about and praying over 1 Corinthians 6:18–19. How can you honor God (and others) with your body? How can you honor God and others with how you dress and present yourself?
- In the area of physical purity, we are all tempted. It is wise to have an accountability partner to check in with us in this area. Who could be your accountability partner?
- If you are uncertain of complete forgiveness for any past moral failure, seek God and get help from a godly, trusted Christian.

- Meditate on 2 Peter 1:3, "His divine power has given us everything we need for life and godliness through our knowledge of him who called us by his own glory and goodness." How does this affect your response to the Lord and any area where you may be struggling?

Chapter 13

Pure in Heart and Mind

Physical purity begins with mental purity. If you're going to avoid temptation—of any kind—you need to be anchored in God's will and His Word. A direct correlation exists between what you and I fill our minds and hearts with, and our ability to see and experience our remarkable God. As the saying goes, "Garbage in, garbage out." In contrast, Matthew 5:8 tells us, "Blessed are the pure in heart, for they will see God." The Greek word used for "see" is *optanomai*—to gaze, with wide-open eyes, at something remarkable. Scripture reinforces this idea:

"I will set before my eyes no vile thing." (Psalm 101:3)

"To the pure you [God] show yourself pure." (2 Samuel 22:27)

"The good man brings good things out of the good stored up in his heart, and the evil man brings evil things out of the evil stored up in his heart. For out of the overflow of his heart his mouth speaks." (Luke 6:45)

Living in purity and integrity allows us to see more of our remarkable God.

Putting Your Heart and Mind Right Helps You "See" God

The Message Bible translates Matthew 5:8 this way: "You're blessed when you get your inside world—your mind and heart—put right. Then you can see God in the outside world." Seeing God means you see more of who He is and what He does. You recognize His deeds, you rejoice in the workings of His kingdom, you recognize His Spirit's promptings, and you realize His transforming power at work in your life and in others' lives. Here are some ways to get your mind and heart "put right."

1. If you have not done so already, humbly admit your need for a Savior.

Believe through faith that Jesus Christ is the Son of God, the Savior of the world. Confess that you are a sinner, ask for His forgiveness, and invite Him into your life to take over. Put Him in the "driver's seat" of your life. That is the starting point.

If you are already a follower of Jesus Christ, then "preach the gospel to yourself every day," as author and Bible teacher Jerry Bridges so appropriately encourages. This is how we live in His grace.

2. Fill your mind with God's Word, the Bible.

The Bible isn't fiction—read it like it really happened! Meditate on it and think about what it says. Joshua 1:8 captures the overall idea: "Do not let this Book of the Law [the Bible] depart from your mouth; meditate on it day and night, so that you may be careful to do everything written in it. Then you will be prosperous and successful." If you want to grow in Christ and see God, this is an indispensible privilege! This week, choose five or ten or twenty minutes and start reading through the Bible a little at a time several days a week. You might want to begin with one of the gospels (Matthew, Mark, Luke, or John). Each time you read, pick out one thing that stands out to you and jot it down. Make it a habit to meet with the Lord, talk with Him (prayer), read His Word, and personally apply it to your life.

Another key to staying pure in heart comes from Philippians 4:8, "Whatever is true, whatever is noble, whatever is right, whatever is pure, whatever is lovely, whatever is admirable—if anything is excellent or praiseworthy—think about such things." Continually reflect on things pure, noble, and admirable. Among these, the Scriptures rank at the top.

My husband Randy testifies that the habit of memorizing a Bible verse or two each week for several seasons rebuilt his thought structures, refocused his emotions, and redirected his will. Not a bad exchange! It can do this for you too. Start with one verse and review it frequently for several days until you know it well. Keep reviewing it and start on another. By the way, someone helped Randy get started memorizing several years ago. Maybe the Lord would have you help someone memorize one verse this week. As we meditate on these verses, it's another powerful way to cultivate purity in heart that helps us see God.

Sometimes we struggle to fill our mind with God's Word. Occasionally we feel distant from the Lord, especially if we let busyness steal our time with Him. In *The Sacred Romance*, Brent Curtis and John Eldredge point out the central place of our heart in the Christian life. However, we can get so busy *doing* Christian things that we begin thinking our *actions* are the key to the Christian life. God values and delights in our *being*, not just in our doing.

When meeting with Him feels mechanical, pick a host of things to simply thank God for. Thank Him that you can think, walk, move your arms, breathe, see, and communicate. Thank Him that you have a place to live, a car to drive, a bus to take, food to eat, and work to do. Realizing all He's done for you can help break the logjam and open your heart to reconnect with Him.

As you get into the habit of taking in God's Word each day, consider reading through the whole Bible over the next 24 months. Get up 15 minutes earlier or find a little time after you get home each day to read three or four chapters. You might want to select a book or two in the Old Testament and read through those, followed by one or two from the New Testament, and then continue this pattern. Remember to read it like it really happened!

3. Talk to God about anything and everything, with thanksgiving.
Pray over all things and concerns in your heart and life. He wants you to pour it all out to Him, and He's always with you, anytime, anyplace.

4. Get rid of any big or little things in your life and heart that are not good or not honoring to God.
In fact, don't just get rid of them, replace them with honorable and edifying things.

5. Be filled with (empowered and controlled by) the Holy Spirit (Ephesians 5:18).
First Thessalonians 5:19 instructs us not to quench the Spirit. That means saying, "No, Lord, I don't want to do that," or not listening when He speaks to us. Ephesians 4:30 tells us not to grieve the Holy Spirit, which we do if we knowingly continue in sin. We're controlled by the Spirit when we're following God and doing what He says (John 14:21).

As we work, with God's grace and by His Spirit, to keep our hearts and minds pure, we will make decisions that honor Him. He will produce the fruit of His Spirit in and through us—things like love, joy, peace, patience, kindness, goodness, faithfulness, gentleness, and self-control (Galatians 5:22–23). In fact, our spiritual power often depends upon our moral purity. The more we live in moral purity, the greater our spiritual power to live for Jesus Christ and His kingdom. The greater our relationships will be as well, making us better friends, boyfriends, girlfriends, husbands, or wives.

MAKE IT REAL
- Why does purity in the heart begin with purity in the mind?
- What role does the Word of God play in living purely?
- How does living in moral purity increase our spiritual power and deepen our relationship with Christ?

- In what one way can you be more holy in your mind and heart for the Lord?
- How can you be more empowered by or controlled by the Holy Spirit?
- Just days before He knew He would be crucified, Jesus prayed this for His followers: "Sanctify them in truth; Thy word is truth" (John 17:17, NASB). The Greek word for sanctify, *hagiazo*, means to make holy, purify, or consecrate. How does the Word of God sanctify us?

Chapter 14

Living with Unmet Desires

Can you relate to any of these?

- My roommate is getting married, and I'm sad at "losing" another friend.
- My cell phone rings, and it's David's number! Maybe he's calling to ask me out. Ugh, he just wanted Josh's phone number.
- Will I have to wait until I'm 35 to marry?
- Will I get the chance to have a family of my own?
- Where do I channel these romantic desires?

For years I experienced these and many more unmet desires. They often bubble up as we try to hold out for real love within the context of our present reality. Relationships come and go, breathing wind into our sails one day and crumpling our hearts without warning the next. Waiting can seem to last forever. Life can seem so unfair.

Because this life on earth is not our true home, we will carry unmet desires until we are at home with our Lord. Our enemy Satan is also adept at attacking us, often in these vulnerable places. A central question then becomes, in the here and now, how do we live for Jesus Christ while bearing very legitimate and heartfelt desires that go unmet? How do we resist the enemy? How do we honor God and press on with our sometimes exciting but often mundane daily lives?

Here are a few ways I learned to deal with unmet desires.

1. Practice active waiting.
You don't have to stop waiting, but you can wait with purpose. As you

wait on the Lord to hopefully bring the right person into your life, be active and not passive. Don't just kill time; live your life fruitfully! God has a purpose for your life right now. Look for ways to serve and do good things for the sake of Christ. He has chosen you to influence and impact others for His glory. John 15:16 says, "You did not choose me, but *I chose you* and appointed you to go and bear fruit—fruit that will last" (emphasis added).

Sarah Mally, in *Before You Meet Prince Charming*, says it well:

"If your single years are spent simply waiting around for Prince Charming, feeling sorry for yourself, and dreaming of being married, your life will be miserable. But if your days are spent serving the Lord, each day will only get sweeter as you abide in His presence, more joyous as you see His plans for you unfold, and more fulfilling as you learn that it is more blessed to give than to receive (Acts 20:35)."[12]

Here are sundry ideas to keep your waiting more active:
- Learn a new skill that you've always wanted to develop.
- Find one person or family to serve this month.
- Explore and develop an enjoyable hobby, whether it's seasonal like softball or something ongoing like photography.
- Take time to pray for your co-workers and those in your neighborhood or apartment complex.
- Get a world map and pray once a month for other countries and nations, for the gospel of Jesus Christ to change lives.
- Choose one professional-development opportunity this year.
- Meet someone new at church and invite him or her to lunch with a few friends.
- Initiate and share your salvation story with someone. Teach someone else to do the same. [See Appendix A to read my spiritual journey and get an idea of how to tell your own faith story.]
- Use some vacation time to go on a short missions trip with a

heart ready to serve and learn.
- Take a class or finish your degree.
- Organize a fun weekend activity for single friends.
- If you are in debt, begin to climb out of it. I recommend Dave Ramsey's book, *The Total Money Makeover*. Remember that if you don't want to marry someone with a lot of debt, you shouldn't be that person either!

Pastor John Piper recommends asking yourself, "For this season of my life, while I am single, what is it about my singleness that could make me especially fruitful for Christ?" Then give yourself to that. Here are more ideas:
- Have a regular lunch date, or a Saturday-morning phone call, with a friend.
- Lead or participate in a group Bible study.
- Pick one new way to get involved at church.
- Invest in another person's spiritual growth. If you're unsure how or where to start, find someone who is doing it and ask them to mentor you. Look at how Jesus did it.
- Read at least two or three missionary biographies.
- Choose one way to help the poor or someone in need this season.
- Memorize a Bible verse. Memorize it with someone. Go hog wild and memorize a whole chapter.
- Join in some type of ministry outreach or start your own.
- Set one or two short-term goals—professional, personal, or spiritual. What would you like to do this year? What is the first step to take?
- Volunteer somewhere.
- Give generously to someone or to a worthy cause.
- Set aside a half-day to be with the Lord. [See Appendix B for ideas on how to spend this time.]

MAKE IT REAL

- How can you live more wholeheartedly for the Lord? Is anything holding you back? If the Lord Jesus Christ was literally sitting in your living room across from you today, what would you say to Him? What might He say to you?
- Of the various ideas listed, or others you may think of, which one or two will you choose to do?

2. Be consumed with Jesus.

George Sanchez, former international ministries director for The Navigators, wrote:

"In my travels around the world and in the counseling I have done, it is amazing how few people I meet who have an adequate understanding of who the Lord Jesus Christ really is. In fact, I would say that ninety-five percent of the problems people have in their spiritual lives and for which they seek counseling are basically a result of a poor understanding of who Jesus Christ is."[13]

The more we are consumed with Jesus, the less we will be concerned with ourselves and our unmet desires. Part of walking with Jesus is accepting suffering as part of that journey. In her book, *Evidence Not Seen*, Darlene Deibler Rose, a missionary to New Guinea, taught me a deep lesson about humbly obeying Christ and clinging to Him in dire suffering.

During World War II, newlywed Darlene survived four years in a notorious Japanese prison camp set deep in the jungles of New Guinea. Before Darlene and several friends were forced into this brutal prison, her missionary husband Russell had been taken at gunpoint and trucked to another prison camp for men. As the Japanese ordered him and other men onto the truck, Russell said to his young wife, "Remember one thing, dear: God said that He would never leave us nor forsake us."[14] It would be the last time she ever saw him.

Darlene wrote that many months later, after receiving news of her husband's death, "The sword of sorrow had pierced deep within me, but He had bathed the sword in oil." The supernatural comfort of the Holy Spirit was real.

Darlene's life continued with more sorrow, anger, and hard questions. At one point during her imprisonment, she was taken to the Kempeitai headquarters, put in solitary confinement, and endured brutal treatment. The Lord's presence and His Word in her heart helped Darlene survive beatings, ulcers, beriberi, malaria, dysentery, and a host of other cruelties. Still, while in solitary confinement, Darlene came to a place where she was troubled that the Lord's presence, which had sustained her very life, was gone. She was left with a spiritual vacuum. She continued reviewing Scripture from memory, as she routinely did, searching her heart. Then she prayed, "Lord, I believe all that the Bible says. I do walk by faith and not by sight. I do not need to *feel* You near because Your Word says you will never leave me nor forsake me. Lord, I confirm my faith; I believe."[15] The Holy Spirit impressed on her Hebrews 11:1, "Now faith is the substance of things hoped for, the evidence of things not seen."

Darlene then understood that her trust was not in feelings or even in moments of delight with the Lord, but in the unchanging person of Jesus Christ. She was assured that her faith rested not on feelings, but on the changeless Savior—*evidence not seen*. More than ever, she knew she could ever and always trust in the Lord. Shortly afterward, Darlene was forced to sign a false confession and faced imminent death. However, God spared her life.

Indeed, our feelings are an important and valued part of our lives. However, our faith does not rest on our feelings. It rests on Jesus Christ and His unshakeable work on the cross and resurrection from the dead.

- Has any unmet desire or issue driven a wedge between you and God?
- What does it mean for you today to "take up your cross daily" (Luke 9:23)? "It is interesting that when Jesus told us this, He was referring to, among other things, the ongoing process of taking ownership of our lives. Spiritual growth is not instantaneous. It's more like an oven, slowly and gradually heating and melting the ingredients together to produce a new person."[16]
- Think about 1 Peter 2:2 (NASB), "Like newborn babes, long for the pure milk of the word, that by it, you may grow." What is a key ingredient for our spiritual growth? How can you feed yourself on the Word of God regularly?
- Is there an area in which you need to not rest on feelings but believe by faith?

3. Let Jesus Christ be the one to complete you.

Over time, I learned to go to the Lord and let Him be my husband first (symbolically), which means to let Him meet my deep need for love, significance, and purpose. I still do today. Colossians 2:10 (NASB) says it well, "And in Him [Jesus Christ] you have been made complete." Through our faith in Him, all of our sin is nailed to the cross and paid in full. Jesus has made you and me whole, complete, and a new person in Him.

The Lord Jesus is your head, your chief and master, the one who satisfies you first and foremost. In *Believing God for His Best*, Bill Thrasher captures this idea of finding contentment in God alone: "We need to let God train us to look to Him alone for our ultimate sense of security and significance. Only in this way will our ultimate sense of well-being not be determined by the presence or absence of a mate."[17]

As an added bonus, as you and I learn to surrender to God, we are also preparing to learn to surrender to one another in the challenging give and take of marriage. That sets the stage for a great union!

<u>MAKE IT REAL</u>

- As you examine your heart, is there something or someone you love more than the Lord? Will you lay it at the feet of Jesus and surrender it to Him?
- Where else may you be looking to have your needs met? Is that bringing true contentment?
- Psalm 16:11 (NASB) says, "In Thy presence is fulness of joy." How will that impact how you seek joy?
- Our job is to stay connected to Jesus, and then He produces fruit in us. Look at John 15:4–5. How can you stay connected to Jesus (the source)?

4. Consider that Jesus Christ had to wait on His Father.

It stunned me when I realized that Jesus had to wait. There were things He wanted to see happen during His time on earth, but He had to wait on the Father's timing.

One example is that Jesus wanted people to be saved and to come to the knowledge of the truth (1 Timothy 2:3–4). Yet He had to wait on His Father's timing and purposes in this. Jesus could have met this strong desire for people to know the true God in numerous ways. He could have called forth more supernatural displays of power, called down angels and commanded them at His side, opened up the heavens to reveal heavenly glory and heavenly beings, or called forth rocks and trees and animals to speak. Instead, Jesus often chose a depth of self-control we little appreciate. His total surrender to the Father and His plan is astonishing.

As you read the accounts of Jesus' life in the New Testament, notice how Jesus lived and the qualities demonstrated by His actions: self-control, waiting, praying, patience, obedience, relying on Scripture.

Out of love, Jesus submitted to the Father, stayed connected with the Father, and did the work of the Father—even while waiting on the Father.

MAKE IT REAL

* In what way can you follow Jesus' example of submission and patience this week? How does staying connected with the Father make a difference in your life?
* Pick one of the gospels (Matthew, Mark, Luke, or John) and read it through. Jot down ways you see Jesus follow the purpose(s) that God the Father had for Him. How can this impact how you live and what you live for?

5. Be willing to live with a measure of loneliness.

The Lord meets us and often reveals more of Himself as we walk through the gate of pain. One of those gates is loneliness. The older I get, the more I learn to accept it, and in an odd way, I expect to meet Him there.

One particular night in a Walmart parking lot, single and in my thirties, loneliness overwhelmed me. Sitting in my car, I wept because a male friend had deceived and hurt me, and I decided my relationship with him was over. Grieving, I cried out, *"Why?"* What surfaced surprised me. I realized that underneath the loss, what I really wanted was to belong. I wanted to belong to someone. As my tears finally stopped and I grew quiet, the Holy Spirit spoke clearly: *"You belong to me."*

Wow! I belonged to God! It recharged me in every way.

In *Passion and Purity*, missionary Elisabeth Elliot describes loneliness as an offering to God:

"God gives us material for sacrifice. Sometimes the sacrifice makes little sense to others, but when offered to Him is always accepted . . . Our offering to Him may very likely be seen as senseless or even fanatical, but He receives it. Jesus received the precious ointment from the worshiping woman although those present thought it a foolish waste. It is a lesson I understood very dimly in 1948, but it has become clearer and clearer the further I go with God.

I have tried to explain it sometimes to people who are lonely and longing for love. 'Give it to Jesus,' I say. The loneliness itself is material for sacrifice. The very longings themselves can be offered to Him who understands perfectly. The transformation into something He can use for the good of others takes place only when the offering is put into His Hands."[18]

Jesus bore the cross of loneliness too. He was single. He knew temptation. He left the sinless, unified Trinity and His perfect heaven to come live with a bunch of humans who were slow to believe. Why the Lord does not always take away our loneliness or rescue us when it seems He should, I don't know. But He tenderly invites us to "Come to Me, all you who are weary and heavy-laden, and I will give you rest. Take My yoke upon you, and learn from Me . . . and YOU SHALL FIND REST FOR YOUR SOULS" (Matthew 11:28–29, NASB). God may not always remove the loneliness, but strangely, within the yoke of Jesus and in the presence of Jesus, there *is* rest.

MAKE IT REAL

- Is anything simmering underneath your loneliness, such as bitterness, envy, anger, or possibly the feeling that God has forgotten you? Ask the Lord to meet you right where you are and reveal Himself in new and deeper ways.
- Would you offer your loneliness as a sacrifice to Him?
- Hebrews 2:18 says, "Because he [Jesus] himself suffered when he was tempted, he is able to help those who are being tempted." How does that impact your response to Jesus?
- What friendship can you invest in, to give and receive love?

6. Make sure your desires do not become demands.

For years I wanted to be taken care of and thought that meant having a husband to provide. (I believe God hard-wired that into female DNA.) Yet I worked and provided for myself for many years, careful not to let my desire become a demand. I had to ask myself, *"Am I willing to let God take care of me right now in any way He chooses?"* The question was easier to answer in light of what we read in 1 Samuel 8.

The people of Israel, God's people, insisted on having a king to rule over them. Having a king as ruler was a common reality then, and the king ensured protection for the people against any neighboring nation who might attack. However, Samuel, the great prophet of the day, had appointed his sons as judges over the people of Israel. Instead of a king, his sons would rule over the people and take care of them. But the people rebelled and insisted, "You [Samuel] are old, and your sons do not walk in your ways; now appoint a king to lead us, such as all the other nations have" (verse 5).

Notice that last phrase, "such as all the other nations have." This is a demand to be taken care of *in a certain way,* in the way they chose, and in the way that all the neighboring nations had. Though Samuel warned against appointing a king, verses 19 and 20 give the outcome: "But the people refused to listen to Samuel. 'No!' they said. 'We want a king over us. Then we will be like all the other nations, with a king to lead us and to go out before us and fight our battles.'"

Keep reading and you will see that Samuel reluctantly appointed a king for the people, King Saul. You will also see the sad and immense consequences unfold. When we make demands of God, we fail to trust Him. That often brings consequences and can circumvent His very best for us.

MAKE IT REAL

- Are you demanding to be taken care of in a certain way right now? In what way? What effect is it having on your relationship with Jesus? With others?

- Meditate on Matthew 6:25–34. How can you trust the Lord to provide for you? What happens to our heart when we choose to trust Him?

7. Work on healthy friendships and healthy dating (which may mean first getting more emotionally and spiritually healthy yourself).

I am a recovering co-dependent. After several years and too much denial, I painfully discovered my chronic people-pleasing tendencies. Finally owning my problem, slowly I worked on it with the support and input of committed friends. Root causes surfaced, such as being afraid of rejection. I began an offensive to identify lies I had believed deep down—things like, *"If you speak your mind, he will leave you."* I worked at replacing these with truth: *"If you tell him what you are thinking, he may not like it or may criticize you or even leave, but that is his issue, not yours. It is his choice how to respond, and his response is not a reflection on you."*

Identifying and saying no to unhealthy people and things, and saying yes to the right people and things, vastly improved the quality of my friendships with men and women. Dr. Henry Cloud and Dr. John Townsend's book, *Boundaries: When to Say Yes, When to Say No, to Take Control of Your Life,* has been a tremendous help along the way.

Cloud and Townsend teach that dating works best between two responsible people. Since dating also carries risks, one's maturity is very important. This implies that some people may not be ready to date, which is perfectly okay since they are still maturing and learning responsibility and godly values. They counsel:

"Many of the struggles people experience in dating relationships are, at the heart, caused by some problem in the areas of freedom and responsibility. By freedom, we mean your ability to make choices based on your values, rather than choosing out of fear or guilt. Free people make commitments because they feel it's the right thing to do, and they are wholehearted about it. By responsibility, we mean your ability to execute your tasks in keeping the relationship healthy and loving, as well as being able to say no to things you shouldn't be responsible for. Responsible people shoulder their part of the dating relationships, but they don't tolerate harmful or inappropriate behavior."[19]

Strive for healthy relationships among your same-sex friends, as well. Part of the quandary of being an older, single adult is that you may be alone much of the time. I chose for years to have female housemates. I also found friends who were open to me being a part of their family's lives. I went to one friend's house for some holidays, attended her son's football games, and spent a weekend with her family in the mountains. Another girlfriend and I had dinner together regularly and took a couple of short vacations together. These friendships helped me feel valued and loved. Several friends helped me think through choices I made, identify people-pleasing tendencies in some areas, and learn to respond differently.

MAKE IT REAL

- In one of your important relationships, how can you respond in a more healthy or responsible way? Are you perhaps taking responsibility for something you should not? Or is there something good that you need to learn to accept and receive?

8. Cultivate a thankful heart.

Are you thankful or do you grumble more than you realize? Maybe you feel thankful on the inside but what comes out of you reflects something different. A grateful heart blesses others.

- Ask the people who spend the most time with you if they think you are thankful.
- How can you express thankfulness to someone this week?
- When you pray today, express thankfulness to the Lord for who He is.

9. Discover your weaknesses regarding love, romance, and loneliness, and find ways to protect yourself.

Does being home alone on Friday nights heighten your loneliness? Does the thought of sitting alone at church keep you from going? Are the holidays difficult for you? If you're a woman, do monthly hormonal changes rev up your longing for romance or make you more susceptible to compromise? Be aware of these triggers so that you can try to avoid them or learn to deal with them.

I used to rent a romantic comedy to get my fill of romance, even if only vicariously. Sighing, I wished a man would love me like that. Yet sometimes romance movies brought out the loneliness inside too much, and I had to take a break from them. Music was the same. At times I could listen to love songs with no problem, but at other times they made me more aware of my aching desire for a man in my life. When this happened, I would take a break from certain music for a while.

Find ways to protect yourself from or to bear your unmet desires. Maybe you need to limit exposure to that man you have liked for a year who is not interested in you. Find activities and hobbies that take your mind off your loneliness. Cultivate strong friendships. We all stumble at times, but the idea is to be prepared and choose things that help. Ask the Lord for ideas.

- Identify one of your weak spots or temptations. Decide now on a plan to protect yourself when it comes again. Consider enlisting the help of a friend or small group. Who could that be?

- Is there something you could avoid that would help lessen a certain temptation?

- Have at least one trusted friend with whom you can be completely honest, someone you feel safe with and who extends grace and truth. This person can also pray with you.

10. Find a mentor and/or mentor someone else.

Scripture reminds us that we were created to be mentored and to mentor others:

"As iron sharpens iron, so one man sharpens another." (Proverbs 27:17)

"And the things which you have heard from me in the presence of many witnesses, these entrust to faithful men, who will be able to teach others also." (2 Timothy 2:2, NASB)

" 'Go therefore and make disciples of all the nations . . . teaching them to observe all that I commanded you; and lo, I am with you always.' " (Matthew 28:19–20, NASB)

Mentoring others is a wonderful, eternal investment in the life of another.

MAKE IT REAL

- Ask someone you respect to mentor you spiritually or professionally for a season. If no one comes to mind, ask the Lord to provide someone to mentor you.
- Who could you mentor this year?

11. Take care of yourself, but focus on more than just yourself.

God calls us, as adults, to take care of our own normal responsibilities, such as earning a living and paying our debts. Galatians 6:5 teaches this functional independence: "For each one should carry his own load."

However, when life throws us something unusual, like a car wreck or the loss of a loved one, verse two instructs us to "Carry each other's burdens." God created us to be relationally dependent, needing to need others. That is humility.

As we rightly attend to our basic needs and responsibilities, God also calls us to be like Jesus Christ and "look not only to your own interests, but also to the interests of others" (Philippians 2:4). As we take care of our basic needs and serve others, the Lord is honored.

MAKE IT REAL

- In what one way can you take better care of yourself or a responsibility you have?
- Are you humbly and genuinely interested in others for their sake, not just to meet your own needs or desires? Ask God to give you a heart like His, a heart for others.
- What is one way you can serve someone or help them out this week?
- In conversations, how well do you listen? In a conversation this week, instead of frequently interjecting your thoughts or changing the subject too quickly, ask the other person a few questions to gain further understanding.

12. Pray.

Author and speaker Beth Moore talks about two foundational aspects of prayer and peace from the Scriptures. First, Matthew 28:18 tells us that all authority in heaven and on earth now belongs to Jesus. All of it. Based on that, will you and I submit to His authority in our life? That is the first key to finding peace. Beth points out, "The key to peace is authority—peace is the fruit of an obedient, righteous life."[20]

Second, after we have submitted to the authority of Jesus and continue to do so, Beth adds, "Without a doubt, avoiding prayer is a sure prescription for anxiety, a certain way to avoid peace. To experience the kind of peace that covers all circumstances, the Bible challenges us to active, authentic prayer lives. Prayer with real substance to it—original thoughts flowing from a highly individual heart, personal and intimate. Often, we do everything but pray."[21]

Early in my Christian life, I lacked understanding of how to pray from the heart, how to simply talk to God. I thought that praying was reciting a memorized prayer. Thankfully over the years I have learned much about praying from the heart and trusting God. Today, praying has become incredibly dear and essential to me. Philippians 4:6–7 (NASB) says it well: "Be anxious for nothing, but in everything by prayer and supplication with thanksgiving let your requests be made known to God. And the peace of God . . . shall guard your hearts and minds in Christ Jesus."

MAKE IT REAL

- Is there an area in which you need to submit to the authority of Jesus? How about in your love life?
- If you are anxious, is there something you are not giving completely to the Lord? Will you give it to Him and trust Him with it?
- During a time of prayer, pray the Word of God back to Him. For example: Psalm 145: 8–9 (NASB) says, "The LORD is gracious and merciful; slow to anger and great in lovingkindness. The LORD is good to all, and His mercies are over all His works." I might pray something like: "Lord, I praise you that you are gracious and merciful. Thank you that you are slow to anger, and that you are loving and kind. I praise you that you are good to everyone, and that you are merciful."

13. Hope again.

In my mid-to-late thirties, hope evaporated as the reality of meeting the husband I yearned for looked bleak. Then a friend, Nathan, said to me, "You seem to think no one will ever come around. Don't give up hope! You are a wonderful woman, and I think there are a lot of men who would love to spend their life with you." Thank you, Nathan, I needed that!

But sometimes it hurts to hope. "Hope deferred makes the heart sick" (Proverbs 13:12, NASB). Hope seems to yield to heartache, disappointment, and cynicism when what we hope for fails to come true month after month, year after year. I had first-hand experience with this kind of heart-sickness. Then one day I noticed the second half of the verse: "But desire fulfilled is a tree of life."

This stopped me in my tracks. Then it reached down and resurrected a flickering in my soul, and I thought, *"Yes, I would like to experience desire fulfilled."* Quietly, tenderly, and sincerely, as a daughter to her loving Father, I simply asked the Lord if I could experience desire fulfilled, in whatever way He wanted. Several years and more struggles would pass before I met my husband Randy, but that day of discovering "desire fulfilled" breathed a spark of new hope in me and radically reoriented my thinking. Hope was rekindled!

My prayer is that your hope will also be rekindled through the touch of your gracious Father. Nothing can separate us from the magnificent love of God in Christ Jesus our Lord. He loves you with an everlasting love. He is altogether worthy. May He revolutionize your heart, and may you never be the same.

MAKE IT REAL

- Is there an area in which you have lost hope? Ask the Lord to give you a tender spark of new life there.
- Zephaniah 3:17 says, "The LORD your God is with you, he is mighty to save. He will take great delight in you, he will quiet you with his love, he will rejoice over you with singing." Insert your name in place of the word "you."

appendices

APPENDIX A

My Spiritual Journey

My husband and I are utterly grateful for God's marvelous faithfulness and kindness to bring us together as husband and wife. We are also committed to walk the incredibly challenging path of married life as imperfect people. However, a truly fulfilling life and marriage flows from another foundational aspect of our individual lives. Since neither marriage nor a spouse can completely satisfy you or me, our soul satisfaction and worth must come from another source. Here is how I discovered that source several years ago.

By all outward appearances, it looked like I would go to heaven. I believed I was a Christian. I was a "good girl." I worked hard and lived morally the best I knew how. My hard-working parents took us eight children to Catholic mass every Sunday. As long as I can remember, I believed in God the Creator of all and knew Jesus Christ was the Son of God who suffered and died for my sins. After He was crucified and buried, He rose from the dead, and He is alive today reigning as Lord of all. I believed the Bible was God's holy Word, yet something was missing.

During high school, though unable to identify it then, I carried an emptiness inside. Yearning for love and acceptance, I excelled in academics and sports and desperately sought to please others. Though not a big drinker, I partied and drank with friends at times. Boys rarely if ever asked me out on dates, so I concluded I was not pretty enough, not good enough, nor popular enough.

My freshman year at Ball State University proved to be a giant, fearful leap since I had seldom ventured far from home. Scared, lonely, and naïve, I somehow survived that difficult year on campus, despite moving three times in five months! One of these moves would change my life.

Five months into my overwhelming freshman year, I finally moved into the dormitory. Vivian was my roommate and we became friends over a few months. I noticed she was clearly different. Not only was she genuinely friendly and interested in me as a person, she talked openly about God! Vivian actually read her Bible and held Bible studies in our room. I left when she had her Bible study, secretly wondering what they did.

Vivian's friends proved extremely likeable as well. Surprisingly, they had fun without drinking. They cared. They were sincere. They talked about God in real and personal ways. Though not understanding it all, I wanted to be around them.

After a few months, Vivian asked if she could share some verses about what the Bible says it means to be a Christian. As I read several Bible verses with her, I discovered that not only was sin doing bad or wrong things, sin also separates us from a holy and loving God. I learned that people try to get to heaven, or "get on God's side," through various means, including attending church or doing good things. That was true of me. But it was Ephesians 2:8–9 (NASB) that rocked my world: "For by grace you have been saved through faith; and that not of yourselves, it is the gift of God; not as a result of works, that no one should boast."

Like a light coming on, I realized that all of the good things I had done were never enough to get me into heaven, into God's kingdom. I started to understand that it was only by faith, by personally trusting in Jesus Christ and His payment for my sins. Revelation 3:20 (NASB) says, "Behold, I [Jesus Christ] stand at the door and knock; if anyone hears My voice and opens the door, I will come in to him, and will dine with him, and he with Me." I needed to "open the door" of my heart and ask Christ in as my personal Lord and Savior. When I asked Jesus to forgive my sin, come into my life, and make me the person He wanted me to be, I found what I was missing—a personal relationship with Jesus Christ!

This spiritual birth, as the Bible calls it, infused incredible, indescribable peace in me. I had always known about Jesus Christ as Savior, but now I *knew* Him personally. He lived in me, in my heart! He gave me eternal life with Him in heaven! I marveled that I did not have to do anything to earn it. I still marvel. Gradually His love overwhelmed me and I learned how to trust this loving Lord. Friends taught me to read, study, learn from, and personally apply the Bible. It was like water to a thirsty soul! God's Spirit continued changing me from the inside out.

Now my personal significance comes from the Lord Jesus Christ and how He views me. It's not about my performance. He loves me and calls me His daughter and promises to be with me always. His forgiveness is complete. The Lord infused new purpose in my life—to know Him, follow Him, and live for His purposes. Now I gladly bow my knee to the Lord Jesus Christ who is Lord of all, for ultimately, He is what our souls long for.

APPENDIX B

How to Spend Extended Time with the Lord

This plan is designed to help you spend two to four hours in fellowship with God. It can easily be modified if you have more time. You'll need your Bible and something to write on. Sometimes I bring a book of hymns/songs too.

15–20 minutes. Find a quiet place with few distractions to be alone. Write down everything that is a concern, issue, question, or struggle in your life today. This helps clear your mind. You will come back to this list later for prayer.

45–60 minutes. Select a book of the Bible, and choose a portion of it—or perhaps all of it—to read through slowly. Sometimes I start by reading a few Psalms and then I read elsewhere. Ask the Holy Spirit to teach you. Think about what you're reading. What do you observe about God? Jot down a few notes, questions, or highlights. If the Lord speaks to you about anything, jot that down too.

15–20 minutes. Take these observations and discoveries and pray them back to God. Thank God and worship Him for who He is.
- If any sin comes to mind, confess it to the Lord.
- Is there anything that the Holy Spirit brings to mind that He wants you to do?
- If you want, worship God with a favorite song or two anytime during your fellowship with the Lord.

30 minutes. Return to your personal list and pray through each item. Pray for anything else on your heart or mind.

Questions to Consider as You Contemplate Marriage

This material is adapted from *Believing God for His Best.*[22] Some questions are used directly, some are adapted, and a few are added.

1. How do you think you and your prospective mate can better serve and obey God together than separately? Are you obeying God now?

2. Can you describe at least three positive and at least three negative characteristics of your prospective spouse?

3. Can you give three reasons why you think this is the person you should marry?

4. Can you give three reasons why this is the right time for you to marry?

5. Ask your parents, or a mentor who knows you well, "What do you think each of us needs to work on in order to have a successful marriage?"

6. How do you feel your personalities complement each other? How do they conflict? Consider both of you taking the Myers-Briggs Type Indicator® (MBTI). It's an excellent tool to learn about personality preferences and how each of you relates.

7. Are you able to genuinely praise the other person in public?

8. What fears and anxieties do you have about marrying this person? Have you shared them with your parents or a mentor you trust? Have you shared them with your prospective mate?

9. How do you handle your anger? How do you handle conflict? Have you seen your prospective mate when he or she is angry? Can you both disagree without getting angry and talk about the issue at hand? Can you listen and ask clarifying questions for better understanding?

10. Have you considered the financial obligations of marriage? Have you talked honestly and specifically about where you both stand financially?
11. Have you discussed children? Do you feel he would be a good father to your children? Would she be a good mother to your children?
12. For women: Do you feel your future partner is a one-woman man? For men: Is she a one-man woman?
13. Are you able to communicate and connect on a spiritual level with this person?
14. Do you enjoy his or her company and conversation? Do you deeply respect him or her?
15. Have you read any books on Christian marriage or parenting together?

Infatuation or Real Love?

Infatuation can lead to real love, but infatuation alone is not real love. One person described infatuation like this: "Infatuation is the emotional impulse of love untested by time or circumstance." Since infatuation is not a solid foundation for a relationship, it is helpful to compare the two. This is adapted from Barry St. Clair and Bill Jones' book, *Love: Making It Last*, pages 18,19.

Infatuation	Real Love
Fall into it suddenly	Grows with time
Wants sex now	Willing to wait for sex
Up and down emotionally	Consistent
In love with love	In love with a person
Fickle	Faithful
Can't eat or sleep	Has proper perspective
Break up at the slightest irritations	Does not panic when problems arise
Emphasizes beauty	Emphasizes character
Gets	Gives
Based on my feelings	Based on other's needs
Self-centered	Self-controlled
Physical	Spiritual

Expects to find happiness	Expects to work at happiness
May feel this way toward more than one person	Feels this way toward one and only one
Possessive	Allows the other person to relate to others
Has an idealized image of the other person	Has a realistic view of the other person's strengths and weaknesses
Avoids problems	Works through problems

notes

Introduction

1 Paula Rinehart, *Sex and the Soul of a Woman: The Reality of Love & Romance in an Age of Casual Sex* (Grand Rapids, Michigan: Zondervan, 2004), 19.

Chapter 1 – At First Glance

2 Oswald Chambers, *My Utmost for His Highest* (Westwood, New Jersey: Barbour and Company, Inc., 1935), 93.

Chaper 10 – Is This "The One"?

3 Eric and Leslie Ludy, *When God Writes Your Love Story* (Sisters, Oregon: Loyal Publishing, 1999), 148.

4 Bill Thrasher, *Believing God for His Best* (Chicago: Moody Publishers, 2004), 116-117.

Chapter 12 – The Fabulous and Freeing Pure Lifestyle

5 Elisabeth Elliot, *Is He a God of Love?*, The Elisabeth Elliot Newsletter, September/October 1992, 2.

6 The List Guy, *Brown Like Coffee* (www.BrownLikeCoffee.com, 2007), 98.

7 Joshua Harris, *Boy Meets Girl* (Sisters, Oregon: Multnomah Publishers, Inc., 2000), 144.

8 Ibid., 144.

9 Rinehart, 118-119.

10 Ibid., 64.

11 Nancy Leigh DeMoss, "Establishing Moral Boundaries" pamphlet adapted from *Singled Out for Him* (Niles, Michigan: Revive Our Hearts, 1998), 6.

Chapter 14 – Living With Unmet Desires

12 Sarah Mally, *Before You Meet Prince Charming* (Greensburg, Indiana: Winters Publishing, 2006), 151.

13 George Sanchez, "Who Will Be Lord?" *Discipleship Journal*, Issue Sixteen 1983, Colorado Springs: NavPress Publishing, 12-15.

14 Darlene Deibler Rose, *Evidence Not Seen* (Harper & Row: San Francisco, California, 1990), 45.

15 Ibid., 155-156.

16 Dr. Henry Cloud and Dr. John Townsend, *12 "Christian" Beliefs That Can Drive You Crazy* (Grand Rapids, Michigan: Zondervan Publishing House, 1994, 1995), 54.

17 Thrasher, 76-77.

18 Elisabeth Elliot, *Passion and Purity* (Old Tappan, New Jersey: Fleming H. Revell Company, 1984), 64-65.

19 Dr. Henry Cloud and Dr. John Townsend, *Boundaries in Dating* (Grand Rapids, Michigan: Zondervan Publishing House, 2000), 27.

20 Beth Moore, *Breaking Free* (Nashville, Tennessee: The Billy Graham Evangelistic Association with permission from Broadman & Holman Publishers, 2000), 70.

21 Ibid., 71.

22 Thrasher, 135-137.

You can contact Sandy (or Randy) Weyeneth at:

Sandy Weyeneth
1118 War Eagle Court
Colorado Springs, CO 80919
719/528-6621
www.loveworththewait.com
Sweyeneth@comcast.net

Other books by Sandy Weyeneth:

Writing Exceptional Missionary Newsletters
available at www.WCLBooks.com